DWELL IN LOVE III

Communion

Jerry K. Paul

Copyright © 2005 by Jerry K. Paul

All rights reserved. No part of this book may be reproduced, stored in a retrieval system, or transmitted in any form by any means, whether electronic, mechanical, photocopy, recording or other, without the prior written permission of the author.

Cover photograph of wood carving by Tilman Riemenschneider taken and provided by the late Karl Anslinger. Permission given by Christof Messerschmidt, Pastor, Evangelisches Pfarramt in the city of Creglingen, Germany.

Published by: *Isaiah Publications*
P.O. Box 31
Pine Level, AL 36065
www.dwellinlove.com

Library of Congress Control Number: 2004195121

ISBN-13: 978-0-9741673-2-9
ISBN-10: 0-9741673-2-0

Printed in U.S.A.

ACKNOWLEDGMENTS

I am deeply grateful to our Heavenly Father and Jesus for the privilege of being the vessel through which these messages were given to assist us in coming to a closer relationship with Them. I appreciate Their limitless Love for us, for only such Love is sufficient to allow us to release our fears and draw us into the infinite realms of Divine Spirit.

I stand in wonder at the many ways the Father finds to bless and provide for us through our brothers and sisters who desire to be his vessels. Many thanks to Lynn Sparrow for her assistance in bringing through the messages and the wonderful spiritual vibration she brings to the process, as well as her time, which she gave with no charge. Many thanks also to Stuart Dean for his patience and expertise with the editing, not to forget that he has never wanted any kind of remuneration for helping. My cousin, Mary Roten, continues to encourage me and help selflessly, not only with proofreading, but with many of the day-to-day demands of life in the project of publishing these books and taking care of my invalid sister. This book would have taken much longer to finish if it had not been for several of my German friends, Claudia and Uwe Wamper, and Ursula Doerner, who donated substantial amounts of money to enable me to hire sitters to help me with my sister more often so that I would have more time to devote to preparing this text for publishing.

FOREWORD

We are living today in the midst of a spiritual renaissance. The flowers of the divine are opening all around us. The long winter of spiritual confinement is ending, and the spring of mystical revelation is upon us. Not since the spiritual explosion of the 6th century B.C.E. when the Buddha, Confucius, and Lao-Tzu lived within sixty years of each other has the Spirit made such a widespread appearance. The readings of Edgar Cayce, Jane Roberts, *A Course In Miracles*, Pat Rodegast's channeling Immanuel, and most recently the succinct and electrifying work, *The Power of Now,* by Eckhart Tolle have shifted those who are open into a radical way of seeing through the eyes of love and oneness. I add the mystic Jerry Paul and his work, *Dwell In Love*, to this list. It too is a divine flower.

The "feel" of the material is similar to that of *God Calling.* As in that classic in which Jesus speaks so personally to two ordinary women, we hear in Jerry's work a voice for God that is gentle, clear, energetic, and nonjudgmental. The voice is also simple and direct, which is always the signature of Jesus. The questions, which guide and shape the work, come from Jerry himself, the human Jerry, who wonders about creation, forgiveness, suffering, and applying the big answers of spirit to the small, stubborn knots of real life. Jerry is simple in a childlike way in that he is willing to ask the obvious and, at the same time, difficult questions which, in truth, often contain the blocks that keep us from receiving the Light transparently. The answers, which constitute the material of this book, work to soften our resistance with clear distinctions, wise proportions, and practical counsel.

As with all profound spiritual material, which of course are words from the realms of Light, *Dwell In Love* needs to be read over and over again, pondered, so that its depths can be found. Or rather, so its depths can find us. Our resistance to direct material from God is rather massive, and while indeed "the veil is growing thinner" the shield of our defensive approach to the Love that we are is still in place. If we can hold Jerry's words of Jesus to our hearts just as we hold someone we love close, over time we will begin to realize that what we thought we understood was only the beginning of a miracle without end. Prophecy again is alive in our land, and the meek are inheriting (and saving) the earth.

Thomas Baker, M. Div., L.C.S.W.
Virginia Beach, Virginia; February, 2005

TABLE OF CONTENTS

Page

Introduction i

Message about the Supreme Being and the Trinity 3

Message about Jesus 31

Message about Communion 49

Message about Forgiveness 75

Message about Creation 95

Communing with a Brother 115

Message for a Friend 123

Message for the Vessel 137

INTRODUCTION

First, in order to prevent any misunderstanding, I would like to clarify that the subtitle of this book, "Communion," does not refer to the sacrament of the Lord's Supper, but strictly to the experience of the Presence of God and the experience of recognizing His Presence, His Spirit, in our fellowman. The purpose in producing this book was to elicit and share with others as much understanding as possible to assist us in having such experiences.

I would also like to explain that the definition of the "Son" has been expanded to mean all created souls who appear to be separate, as a result of what is called the Fall, but who really are only one Child of God. Through the experience of communion we come to realize our oneness with God and with our brothers and sisters. The messages of this book make it clear that forgiveness is the key to communion, which is itself our salvation.

When God created His one Son (Child), the process was one of extending a part of Himself, rather than making something that would be separate from Him. The Fall could be defined as a decision by the Son to fantasize that He is separate from God, and this decision resulted in the creation of the physical universe in which separate bodies would serve to support this illusion of separateness. But God's true creation was not undone or ruined by this fantasy—it only appears to be hidden by the fantasy because, through identification with physical bodies, we came to rely on physical senses to bring us knowledge of reality. Through communion, which comes about by means of forgiveness, we awaken from the spell of the fantasy and begin to identify with our true spiritual selves—and spiritual sight is then restored.

It cannot be emphasized enough that the imagination plays a very important role in forgiveness and communion, because in order to commune, we must set aside our human, mental faculties of judgment and perception and identify with the spirit within us. In order to do this we must substitute holy and perfect images of other people for the unholy and imperfect ones we have made with the discriminating mind. Once we have imagined this perfection (this is what forgiveness is), then the door is wide open for communion to take place. Spiritual sight then flows across the holy image, and there is an experience of oneness and perfection—of holiness. We realize that there is nothing except God, and perceptions of other than that are as a mirage that dissolves.

Jerry K. Paul

Message About the Supreme Being and the Trinity

THE SUPREME BEING AND THE TRINITIY

nly true that we on earth have sufficient tasks, re-
ies, and problems to keep us busy that we don't
overly concerned with things far beyond the mat-
d; however, those of us who love God really do
ow Him better. We ask God to tell us about Him-
have speculated that there is not really one Su-
ng who is the source of all that exists. Would God
ut Himself before all creation took place?

*er and ever. I exist before all creation, and I exist
. I am the source of all Light, all Love, all En-
verything that has been created. My Being cannot
hended by your earth mind; however, My Spirit
within you feels and knows Its kinship with Me, and It desires
to realize, to experience, Its coexistence with Me—to know*

Itself as a part of Me. It desires to understand the origin of Itself, and it is only natural that It should desire to do so. I exist as Being, Pure Being—always—and yet, within that Being was a desire to create, to create perfectly by creating that which is, always was, and always will be Myself—to create Myself manifest and expressed, for this is My great joy. Creation is My Love having a chance to express Itself towards other parts of Myself in creation, recognizing Myself, and having joy in that—having joy in the diversity (the manifold aspects of that creation). And the Love dances with joy in the Light that is limitless, has no end, can never be exhausted.

*In this Divine Play of My Light and My Love you also came into existence, and as you desire to know of this, you come closer to experiencing and comprehending to some extent— actually, to remembering— that which you are and ever will be. And as you remember, you no longer need to understand, for you remember what **is**—you remember Me, you know Me, you recognize Me; and as you do so, you feel That within yourself That is identical with Me welling up within your heart and rejoicing in the recognition that here is nothing other than you—you, Myself, and all else that is created in the* *same way. You recognize the beauty, the purity, of all that is, and you recognize that you are forever safe in My Heart because that is where you are—you exist in My Heart. And you also recognize My Joy in you, My Joy in seeing Myself as you—always perfect, always filled with love, and radiating a light that brings great joy to all who can see and know it.*

And so, my child, as you desire to know Me, you are desiring to know yourself, for in recognizing Me, you recognize yourself, and the joy causes you to leap and dance, and laugh as you embrace all other creation. You come and melt into My Heart, and then spring forth again into creation, rejoicing in every embrace—putting your arms around your brothers and bringing them with you to melt again into Me so that you may know the source of your creation and go back again with your brothers, dancing and laughing, and allowing Me through you to continue the creation process. And you also recognize the Joy that I have in seeing you playing in the Light, dancing in the Love, and returning periodically to embrace Me.

My dear child, I have great Joy in your interest in knowing about this, for it allows you to be a perfect creation—allows

Me without hindrance to create through you—for those who have (for a short period of time) forgotten about Me and forgotten their true identity are for a short time without that joy. But part of your function is to help awaken that within them—to gently lift the scales from their eyes, to reach forth and touch the heart of each one: to quicken that heart, reminding it of the joy within so that it will desire to remember—allow you to take it by the hand and turn its gaze back towards the Light; allow you to part the clouds in its awareness (its earthly consciousness), to part those clouds so that it may begin to get a glimpse of that Light and to feel the Love whence it came; and then spring with joy and say, "Take me further! I want to return so that my joy may be full and my heart may be fully open to expressing this Love—and I in turn may extend It to others myself." And then that one returns with you, and you have your arms around each brother as you bring him to Me.

You look into the Light, for now your eyes can bear it, and your heart is open fully to that Love. And as you return, you say, "Father, I come with one *so* beautiful, so that we may both have joy in him, and I ask You: prepare him that he may *now enter into Your Heart and be free of all those clouds so that he may commune with You, and when he has forgotten all the anguish and sorrow that was once his experience—when he has forgotten—he will return again laughing, dancing, and filled with love—and desire to also go forth and find another to inspire and bring back himself to Your Heart." This is your function, and even though some may say that your function is only to dance in the Light and send forth Love, deep within you know that part of your function is to go forth gathering unto you and bringing to Me those who have lost the vision, so that you may beam forth Light from your countenance as you see them released from those clouds and returning to Me. This is your function. This is also your choice, and it must be chosen of your own free will. I would not force it upon anyone, but those who desire to know in fullness My Light, My Love, My Being, will surely recognize that this choice is innate in that desire to know Me. For you could never feel whole, complete, and full in your joy and love knowing there was one floundering about in darkness, feeling lost, not knowing the way, and crying out, "Father, if You exist, send someone to touch me, someone to embrace me so that I may know love again—someone to guide me."*

Can we commune and have a relationship with the Supreme Being? If so, how?

You have been taught, "Love the Lord God, with all your heart, with all your soul, with all your mind, with all your being," (Deut. 6:5) and that love opens doors, but My dear child, not all of your brothers are capable of loving Me totally at this point as they wander in darkness, and yet, they need only cry out for help. Still, you must understand that some don't even cry out. Those who cry out, and who weep in sorrow, have an advantage over those who have become so fascinated with the outer expressions of creation that they have no desire for anything more, and yet, they must also be awakened. You have as part of your function to pray for their awakening, and you must understand, and also accept, that (for some) they must first become disillusioned with creation—even experience some pain and have an intense feeling of being lost and lonely before they will cry out. You must have patience with this process and know that this pain, the suffering, the anguish, that wrenches your heart is a blessing that will open the doors so that they may desire to commune with Me.

Once they ask for this and have turned on their pathway back towards the Light, then know that an immediate communing with Me at that point is not possible, but I send to them my vessels so that they may know in some limited way at first—that they may know in part—My Love by the love you express towards them, which may in the beginning be just a touch on the shoulder or a question, "How are you today?" And as they begin to allow expressions of love, they may allow you to embrace them—even in the physical form—but perhaps before that they may allow you in spirit to come to them and embrace them. But your patience must be without limits. You must continue to come to the doorway of the heart of your brothers. You must speak to them gently, and even though they may have in the past rejected you, or feel in their earthly consciousness that it is not fitting to express love—that this is a sign of weakness, or perhaps they fear expressing love (fear that they may be harmed or suffer)—you must stand there in your infinite patience, speaking to them gently, that is, allowing Me to speak through you. In your earthly consciousness you do not know what words, what deeds, would touch them in the beginning. You must always ask Me, "Father, show me, speak through me, touch through me, help me to always be empty, pure, undefiled, so that You may without limitation touch my brothers through me. And should I ever allow something to come between You and me—some slight veil—purify me in whatever way is necessary (burn away the dross), for I have desire that not one thing should be in me that would cause a delay in my brother knowing the joy of rejoicing and dancing in the Light."

So, as you come each time (over and over again) to your brother, you are yourself preparing him or her for that communion of which you speak. And as they begin to trust you and allow you to put your arms around them, or take them by the hand and bring them with you, you are also hastening the day when they know in fullness who they are, whence they come, and in whose arms they rest. Then, as your brothers allow those things to be lifted, and they themselves desire to come, you will see that, as with yourself, the communion only takes the desire to direct your thoughts away from those things in your mundane life that distract—to release those apparent problems and conflicts, and gaze upon My Light and My Love in their hearts. Then as you turn to Me, you experience and know Me as I am—you experience yourself in unmanifested form—and you know not only the Light and the Love, but also the serenity of True Being, which can just rest within Itself—and yet still is radiating Holiness in all directions. This communion is a gift and is part of the manner in which I create, for That which is Myself can always commune with Me and know Itself.

Is there a Trinity? If so, what was the purpose of this apparent division?

Once I desired to know Myself and My creation, I sent forth great waves of Light and Love and Energy so that I might know this as Myself extended forth, and the forms that resulted from this are manifold—without number. All of creation radiates My Light and Love, and as this goes forth through the vast reaches of time and space, there are more and more dense levels. My children have sometimes become so fascinated with this expression of Light in the forms, that they have tended to become lost (tended to forget that they rest in this Light and Love), and at times have experimented with Light and Energy—even experimented in ways that were not extensions, but were an attempt to mold the energy into forms perceived as being apart from themselves and Myself. As a result of this, there has been a need to see—a need in the sons of God to perceive and see—the Father, the Ultimate Creative Force, as Itself expressed in different forms. There is a perception of Myself as being divided, but know, My child, all realizations of Myself are also recognized as belonging together.

There is a perception of Me as a Father by those who feel a need for a father's love, and who also need to see this expression of love coming forth from the Creator. Then there is a perception of Myself as having a separate expression as Spirit, indwelling all that is created and knowing Myself as a source of infinite wisdom (wisdom about creation)—Spirit (Myself) as a person to whom one could turn and ask how the creative forces manifest, and for an understanding of these forces, as well as how the sons may harmoniously express with and through these forms. And then, there was also a need, a desire, to perceive Me as the manifest Son—to perceive the Son as a unique being. And so, this Trinity serves a purpose—serves a divine purpose—for the sons. It brings them comfort, and also brings assurance to the mind that desires to understand. I can be approached through any aspect of the Trinity, and do bear in mind that some of the sons feel more affinity with one of these aspects than with the others, because each son is itself unique, and manifests and expresses uniquely—some accentuating more the aspect of one part of the Trinity than another.

Are the three Persons different from the Supreme Being? If so, in what way?

The three Persons are expressions—expressions in different ways. One expression is more of a creative Person concentrating more on sending forth energy and forming it, mingling it, with other energies into the manifold forms of creation. This is called by you the Father, progenitor of creation. Then after the creative process there is the Spirit of understanding of the Law, in understanding how all things work together in harmony—not in conflict. And the Spirit also brings comfort. It brings knowledge—it brings knowledge of the Trinity and knowledge of the Supreme Being. And It goes forth throughout all creation and is accessible to all who will turn and say, "I desire to know and understand to the extent that is necessary in order for the Father to perfectly express through me, and I desire also to know the Father." And yet, there are those who cherish and delight in the idea of the Father as a Son—a Son with whom one perhaps more easily identifies because one can turn to the Son and say, "Help me to look to You and be able to see a mirror of myself—to see how I was truly created. And I can identify with a Son because it is more a spirit of brotherhood, of being a brother, which may be less intimidating, and also because I can see the Son as an intermediary." This is also a great comfort to the children of God.

Is there more to be said on why we feel separate from God and from each other on earth?

It is truly not easy being born on earth and growing up hearing of the interpretations that all the other beings you encounter have of what creation is and what you are. This makes it very difficult. It requires, in order to go beyond this, that you inquire and have a great desire to know, or feel within yourself—deep within the heart—a desire to commune with, to know, that which you truly are and whence you came, because it is so easy to look with the eyes of the body, to listen with the ears of the body, to perceive only forms, and to even doubt that there is a reality beyond. And yet, it is your salvation to do so. But there is not a need to feel lost or to feel that you are not capable of doing this. In My infinite Wisdom, in My unlimited Love, I send forth to you—to each one—an expression of Myself to touch and awaken, to beckon, to embrace in whatever way is possible, and it is always necessary that these vessels be empty, that they not imagine they have the wisdom to know how all this should come about, but simply be empty—to allow Me to flow through, to ask Me to flow through. And as this happens then they truly do know Me. So, the earth and the inhabitants upon the earth have gone through much suffering, and violence, and darkness. All upon the earth have groaned at times, but it is a perfect and holy process. You are not forgotten.

Bear in mind that sometimes those who have fallen the lowest, who sink into the mire of darkness, are those who will rise to the highest peaks, for in knowing the depths, you become capable of desiring and knowing the heights. But even those who are not conscious of the depths are not forgotten, and their sleep will come to an end. They will be awakened and will also desire to know—as they see more and more brothers filing past them toward the Light, they will begin to wonder and desire to know: "Where are these beings going who are laughing and dancing, and radiating love?" And that will become contagious, and they will ask, "May I go with you?" And you with joy will embrace them and say, "Of course, I take you with me." As you gather them together and bring them to Me, you will always desire to return to see if there is still one soul left wandering there not knowing where to turn, and these you will also bring. And you will realize that the darkness that seemed a curse—the suffering that made you lose heart—was itself a blessing, and it opened a door to returning to Me—to communion. (Perhaps there are those sons you are not aware of who still remember their connection with Me, even if not consciously, but who are very much engrossed with creation, and who may have a desire not quite so strong to return periodically for an embrace; but you, My child, have that desire, and you will recognize that it *was the **ordeal** you **endured** that has brought you into My very arms—into My embrace—and it has been your blessing.)*

Are we to understand that the earth is not in trouble and that this is the normal developmental pattern for a planet?

Not every planet goes through these processes in this way, and although earth may be perceived to be in trouble, and certainly has brought itself into a state that has caused much suffering to be experienced, it also has opened a doorway— for any misdirection contains within it the answer to the correct direction. The earth is in a process of releasing some of the negativity and journeying back towards the Light, but by no means was it ever without hope, and by no means was it ever going through something that was not a process to a tremendous blessing.

What should we on earth be striving, or working, towards?

It is very important that those of you upon earth not forget, but rather remember, that it is a part of your function to desire to know the Father—to return to a conscious experience of this Love and Light, and to a knowing of your true identity—*however, there are other parts of your function, and you must participate in the process, the activities, all the goings-on on earth that present themselves to you. For, in order for you to fully fulfill your function, you must take part in the progressive journey from darkness toward Light as it takes place in the lives of those among you, as well as in the earth itself, and all creation on earth. You must in many physical ways participate in even the most dense procedures of washing away the darkness and bringing forth the Light within. So, you must participate in the political aspects of your countries. You must be concerned about the ecology, the animals, the plants upon earth. You must be truly concerned about helping those who have not even the basic necessities of life, and about the educational processes of those who are learning to live the life on earth, as well as helping them to learn of the Divine Spirit within. So, you must balance your time and your energy. And you must take quiet time to commune with Me.*

You must withdraw from the inner contentions and conflicts of your lives, to recognize Me in the heart of each brother. And then you must also go and offer proposals to help those who may not yet be capable of understanding the spiritual aspects—to awaken in them a desire to be concerned for those around them and to put themselves into the shoes of others who are suffering—and you must accept to offer every possible kind and helpful deed. For you have not truly fulfilled your function to the highest if you close yourself off and say, "This is for someone else." You may truly commune with Me and go forth into the marketplace, into the highways, and see someone who is truly in need of your sharing that which is of monetary value or something that may be food to eat. And even in doing so you may be on your way to a university where you again share ideas that lift the hearts and minds of those around you further towards the Light. Each day, ask, "Father, help me that I may be open and empty, and help me also to recognize each opportunity You present to me," for you may have 100 opportunities in one day. Desire and ask that you be helped not to neglect anyone, not to pass even one by. In so desiring and asking, you do your part in hastening the day when your brothers no longer wander in darkness, but dance in the Light.

Is there more that can be said on how each one of us can best fulfill his or her function on earth?

As you ask for Me to inspire you, to help you, to give you opportunities, bear in mind that you may sometimes have had ideas come to you, and you think, "This is what I must do today." Always be willing and ready to have Me change your direction for the day, to have Me perhaps delay your plans, or just simply add another aspect. And if your progress on a certain path for the day is blocked, then turn within and say, "Father, lead me in whichever way is Your intention for the day. I release the former plans and know that You will open that again if it is Your will. For I know that Your will is my greatest happiness and joy, and it is also that of my brothers.

Can we commune with and have a relationship with God the Father, if so, how do we best do it?

The aspect of My Being known as the Father is a great comfort for the sons of God, My children—in particular for those who have lost a sense of conscious identification with Me, but also those who seek a sense of security and a love such as that of a parent, of a father, of one who takes responsibility for each one, of one who can be approached simply by their thinking of the Father and speaking (whether speaking softly within or with the lips). Simply imagine in your mind that there is a Heavenly Father, One whose Love is without limits and One who does not withhold His Love—no matter how far you may perceive yourself as having strayed away from the relationship or strayed away from following the precepts and laws of holiness. The process is simple: just think of Me, the Father. Speak, speak of what is on your heart. Tell Me your troubles—that which brings you anguish, that which causes you to suffer, even physically. Speak to me, knowing that I am your Father, that I listen with Love, and that I hold you in My arms. And once you have brought your troubles to Me, then accept that you can release them there and depend upon Me to bring about that which is holy, that which is pure, that which is perfect—and also that which is loving. But also accept that you cannot yourself know the solutions to your perceived problems—you cannot know in your limited consciousness (in the consciousness of your reasoning mind or your emotions, or in your feelings of the need to defend and preserve your being against other forces). Of yourself you cannot understand and know.

Occasionally there are things that must be released by you, and at times you will not release your clinch on them unless there is some stress that causes you to release. So, as the situations come to you and you come to Me, then ask to be helped, and accept that I know what is best, and I will bring things about in the best way and at the best time; and you can truly have the feeling of security and belonging as with your Father, for I am That. Come, trusting, allowing Me to arrange all things for My child in whom I always have pleasure and joy. My joy is heightened when you turn to Me rather than looking away from Me unto those things that do not truly help.

Is there a way of knowing when we should turn to God, the Father, or when we should turn to another Person of the Trinity for help?

All Persons of the Trinity are parts of Myself, perceived by you as being different. You may turn to that Person of the

Trinity with whom you might feel a greater affinity—turn to that Person who feels more comfortable to you at that time. However, come to the Father with all your concerns about your well-being, your sense of alienation, and the apparent conflicts with other brothers, so that I may lovingly show you the truth about yourself and, when you are willing, the truth of who your brother is.

As to the Person of the Holy Spirit: often there are those among you who would turn, seeking understanding and wisdom, seeking those things the mind would know—seeking to better understand My creation and how you can commune with and function harmoniously with all parts of it, as well as to understand how different aspects of creation function so that you may then rejoice in the myriad forms you see around you—and the different aspects, functions, and purpose of each one of them.

Then as to the Son: the Son is the Person of the Trinity who has come forth from the Father delighting in being of the Father—the Father Himself. And for those of you who may seek a more personal relationship in the sense of a companion who you, in your present state of limited consciousness, might feel would be more understanding of you, of whom you would have a better understanding, and with whom you would have a better companionship, then turn to Him. For the Son is that which you are, and as you continue to pursue these relationships and this understanding, you will understand that you are also identified with the Son—the Son in creation looking always back to the Father, and yet looking into creation and seeking to create within the framework of the Father's will (that which is perfect). The Son helps you to understand this, and you feel the companionship when you speak to Him as though speaking to an Elder Brother—one who can teach you of the Father, even through example. And yet, my child, always remember, the Supreme Being is also accessible to you. It is just a matter of your being able to accept this. For there are those among you who fear that which is divine, and they are offered different ways in which they may approach and come closer—and then also come to understand the relationship with the divine and the purity of their own being.

For those whose experience with the earthly father has been of a negative nature, is it best for them to simply not concern themselves with God, the Father, or should they make an extra attempt to commune with God, the Father, to repair that wounding?

For some the approach could be best through that of the Son—the feeling of a holy friendship—and the Son can also help in healing the relationship with the earthly father so that those who are troubled by those relationships come to understand that the Father-nature, in and of itself, is always pure and holy, but the physical father may have been seeking himself and had perhaps not found the relationship with the Heavenly Father. And those experiences with him that were of what you would call a negative nature were simply an expression of his floundering about, not knowing how to find that secure and holy feeling—and the infinite Love. And so, the Son, the Holy Son, that Person of the Trinity, can help you with this so that then you may also approach the Heavenly Father trusting that all is well, you are safe, and there is nothing to fear.

It has been said that the three facets of the Supreme Being correlate to the three dimensions of this plane. Are there more than three facets to the Supreme Being in the higher dimensions?

The three facets within the higher dimensions are themselves perceptions of a division of the Supreme Being, but they also serve different purposes in creation. There is the Father of creation. There is also the Father who secures and preserves things in creation until the time has come when the forms no longer serve a purpose. And then there is the aspect of returning all those back to the oneness, whence it can once again go forth into creation serving a purpose ordained by Him.

Is there a closing message about God the Father?

Understand, that the door is never closed. The Father can always be reached. The decision is yours, and the time that you reach out depends upon your choice; but the Father is always there, and there is no barrier. All barriers perceived by you are brought about by your own feeling of guilt and alienation for having turned away from the holiness from which you come, and what you need is to release the guilt. I assure you, you need only turn. I am always there.

Is there a closing message from or about the Holy Spirit?

For those who have great interest in understanding how creation came about, how it exists, how it expands, and the laws that were put into force, come, inquire. The Holy Spirit contains all the wisdom you need to help you to participate harmoniously with the creation of the Father. Come, asking to better understand so that you may work with creation and be a part of it—not coming to understand how you may use knowledge of these laws for a personal benefit, excluding others; for exclusion does not exist in the Mind of God. All is included in Its Oneness.

Is there a closing message from or about God, the Son?

I walk with you everyday, wherever you are, for I am in your heart. You are a part of the Son. You are a part of the creation of the Father—that creation through which the Father can observe and have joy in That which is of Himself,

That which is Holy. And so, turn to Me as that friend, that brother—One who understands, and One who walks with you. Speak with Me as you walk down the street, as you drive in your car, as you walk on the beach or in the woods, and you will truly know the Son in all gentle love walking with you, speaking to you of the Father. Just simply ask and believe. The Son is with you.

MESSAGE ABOUT JESUS

MESSAGE ABOUT JESUS

How is Jesus related to God the Son?

Those upon earth wandering in confusion, and many in darkness, asked for One to come—One who was pure, One who was holy, but also One who could come and identify with them so that they might feel that He is approachable. And so this One, this beautiful Son, came to exemplify the Love of the Father—coming as an expression of the Son; coming as one to reveal the Son on earth and to give you the example of what you can become, or better said, come to express; coming as One to help you to recognize your true nature so that you may then express as the Son coming forth from the Father, knowing with confidence that you do come forth from that Heart of Love; coming as a beam of Light that was so pure and holy that it danced in its joy. He came to remind you of those things you had forgotten, and it was with great joy that He accepted this charge, this mission, even though He knew that Love personified and expressed would also cause a reaction from those who had turned away and closed themselves off.

*He knew that the experience would not always be easy, and that as He looked upon those who suffered, it would at times cause Him to weep. He came, accepting all that, with a mission to exemplify—for on earth you need the example. Just to read a text that tells you of these things is not sufficient for many who have lost hope, but to have an example **brings** hope—an example of One they can look upon with great love and admiration and say, "Oh, Father God, I would be as this One. Help me that I may become so pure—that I may also be such a One." Such hope was given—a hope so great that it did not die in two thousand years. The joy He had and expressed still touches those who read of Him, who think of Him, who speak to Him and ask Him to come and be with them. This was a great star of hope for the earth, and because of this He remains very closely associated with the earth and its development. He stands always there, opening ways and protecting the flickering flame that has been lit in one who cannot yet walk without stumbling, so that the flame will not* *be blown out, and the stumbling one will always have someone to lift him up—that he not feel that those who are lost are depriving him of his birthright.*

So, He came. There was much joy in heaven and much anticipation and joy on earth. For those on earth who asked and believed that it could be true, that it could come about, opened the doorway for the entrance of this beautiful Son to come and express Love, to embrace His brothers, to beckon to them, to put His arms around them and lead them gently back to the Light of the Father. And in so doing, He also set the example of One who cares for all parts of the being—One who does not just come, preach and give concepts, and then retreat to His mountain top, but One who walked among those who suffered, who gave kindness to those in need, who gave food to those who were hungry, and who touched those who were suffering from illness so that they might know the Father is concerned about all their cares—all their needs—and also that they might know it is fitting to always turn to the Father with every need. For this One would never have you think that it is beneath the Father to be concerned with where your daily bread comes from; that you have shelter from the *elements of nature; that you have that with which you clothe your body; or that you have companionship with those of like and similar nature (those who also seek to know the Father) so that you not feel alone; and also that you know and come to realize that you may commune with the divine in the heart of your brother—and in so doing come to respect and appreciate your brother, and to look past all those appearances that have blocked your view in the past. For as you gaze upon the purity in his heart, and you see the Holy Light and accept to receive the Love of the Father there—the love of the Divine—then you know the Father expressed through another one, and in so doing you forgive (you release all your judgments). And a peace comes upon you that you have never known before, a peace you cannot understand, a peace that allows you to go forth into the confused and conflicted world around you without fear, knowing that when you accept to be the expression of the Father—to be the **vessel** of His expression—that there is nothing to fear and all things are taken care of, so that you may without fear go wherever there may be a brother reaching out for a helping hand, for a touch, for an embrace from one who truly cares and who understands.*

You mentioned great joy in heaven and on earth at His birth. Are there other circumstances surrounding His birth that would be important for us to know?

For those who had eyes to see and ears to hear, (see Matt 13:9 and Mark 8:18) there was truly an expression of Divine Light and songs of joy from heavenly realms—Light to be seen, songs to be heard—and it made the heart leap, knowing that the Father cared for those on earth, and there was a blessed event—One who was coming to teach of that which is the salvation of those on earth. And those who watched Him as He grew in stature, and who could see and could hear, knew there was something deep and divine within this One. There was a knowing of heavenly things, even as He went about His many chores, attending to the tasks of a child who cares for His father and mother on earth and for his brothers and sisters. And as adolescence was upon Him, at times great words of wisdom came forth from His lips, and those who were not too arrogant to accept that such wisdom could come from a child gazed in wonder and gave thanks to the Father in heaven for the mercy He had shown to the inhabitants of earth.

And then as His mission came to fruition, came to its fullness, there was no doubt that there was a Divine Radiance—a Light to be seen by those with a pure heart, those who desired to follow in the ways that would bring them in closer relationship with the Divine (with the heavenly things). They saw the Light; they knew the loving kindness that is only from higher realms; and they heard the voice that expressed kindness and love, but almost seemed to be a voice of music—in particular, when he laughed, it seemed heaven laughed with Him. Through example He taught, and also through stories He tried to help those around Him understand. Yet He looked upon the ones who saw Him as a threat as children of God who had allowed a cloud to be drawn about them, to be drawn close to them—a cloud that did not allow them to perceive the Light and the Love. And He prayed to the Father for them that the scales might be lifted from their eyes, and spent many hours communing with the Father and asking, "How can I allow You through Me to touch even these?" But as they plotted against Him, He also realized that no matter what they planned in their hearts, it could serve a divine purpose, and it could be the instrument through which even greater revelations came.

And so it was, even as they planned to put an end to His earthly life, His earthly personality did look with some misgivings upon the prospects, but He came to the Father and said, "Your Will be done, and I would allow this deed of theirs to be the instrument through which My brothers see that One who knows the Father and rests in His Heart also knows He has nothing to fear; that what they might do to the outer shell in no way compromises the spirit within, but provides an example to them of One who continues to reach forth and attempts to touch the hearts of those in darkness, and continues to say, 'Father lead me to a way, or show me a way that I may touch,' and that One who is anchored in this knowledge of the Father does not condemn, but even as they are going about their violent deed, says, 'Father, forgive them of this—they don't understand.' And I desire that one day they may truly understand and may participate, even in this event, so that all may know that this is truly the manner in which a Child of the Father walks the earth and takes part in the events around Him, and fearlessly goes about that task the Father had given—that **opportunity** the Father had given—to assist those wandering in darkness." And this Joy, anchored deep within His heart and soul, this Light and Love of the Spirit, allowed him to walk through this event identifying with the Spirit within, blessing those around Him—even one who was also experiencing a similar event, one hanging on a cross beside Him who called out and said, "May I be with You today in paradise?" And in spirit He reached out and embraced this one, and lifted him away with Him into the perfect resolution, the perfect outcome—into the freedom of purity and holiness.

And being a Pure and Blessed Son of the Father, He continues to this day going about doing this. There is not a single soul who would call to Him and would not have His Presence—His Loving Presence—there. Even though in their earthly consciousness they may not yet be at a point where they might recognize such, still the heart that believes allows the darkness to be lifted to a certain extent so that it does receive an experience, in part, of the Love that is extended towards it, and receives, to whatever extent it can at that time, a peace—a peace it cannot explain or describe. And this gives *it hope to go forth the next day and to ask again, "Help me through the situations this day, and help me when I am so tortured that I cry out against my brother, and I curse him, so that I may then afterwards remember that this is one who cries out as I do—that I might then say, 'Father, now convert that event in which I cursed my brother into one in which he is blessed. Now I ask you, lift the scales from my eyes that I may see You there in his heart; that I may be blessed by seeing Your Holiness, Your Light; that I may feel Your Love. And I ask that my brother on whom I gaze receive nothing less than that which I receive, and that my cursing of him be turned into a blessing of the highest order so that this opportunity You gave to me, and I at first did not recognize, may now be an opportunity that can be fulfilled in its fullness.' And now that one whom I had despised in my ignorance, I put my arms around, and I come before You and I say, 'Bless us together so that we may know You—that we may have the joy of knowing the Presence of Holiness, of seeing a Light that would blind us in our ignorance, but as we turn towards You, You allow us to behold. Bless us both so that we may know that Love, and bless us as your vessels—that we may go back into the world, and that we have the intention to always recognize the Light in our brothers, but should we allow ourselves to be deceived by a perception of a personality, again turn that into an opportunity of recognition of holiness.'"*

*So, the Blessed Jesus walks the earth inspiring us everyday, and we look to Him always as the teacher, the guide, the master—and yet as the Elder Brother who is always approachable—and no matter how we feel that we have sinned, and how defiled we may feel, we know that He looks through that mask—that cloud around us—and sees the Father's Heart within us, and always greets us with an embrace that causes us to release our perceptions of what we are, and of what our brothers are. And we give thanks to the Father for this One who came to change earth from a place of suffering and darkness to one that allows more and more Light to come in, so that it is transformed into a place of joy, a place of love, a place where heaven is, for those who will allow it to be. We thank You, our Holy Brother, Jesus, that you dwelt among us, that you **dwell** among us, and that we may count You as our dearest friend. Thank you! We embrace you!*

We ask for a message from Jesus to those on earth.

My life upon the earth was an example to you. I came to be your brother. I came not to be worshipped, but to be One you turn to and you trust as your brother. I would have you go forth into the world following the example I gave: looking upon your brothers and perceiving their fears, their ignorance, but seeing it only as a cloud that can be lifted—and knowing it is a matter of their ignorance being lifted, and being replaced by knowledge of Truth, knowledge of the Holiness of all creation—and that this comes about by your acknowledgment and your expressions of the appreciation you have of that purity within. I would have you follow My example of assisting your brothers in all ways that are appropriate, and whenever you may wonder what might be appropriate in any circumstance, just ask Me, and I will guide you. I will put the words into your mouth, I will give you the impulse to move, to go, to touch; and I will allow you, if it is the greatest blessing for your brothers, to also alleviate the physical pains, sufferings, and needs to whatever extent is appropriate and helpful to them—bearing in mind that there may be some limitation to what you may be able to do because it may be that some brother may need a little hardship of his own in order to identify with other brothers with hardships—and in order to seek to know the Father.

When you look upon a brother, and you know that there may not be something that you may be able to personally do on a physical level, you may always look upon his heart and ask, "Father, help me recognize You in this brother, and in that recognition have such joy that I embrace him." And be assured that the love you offer will not fail to be delivered to your brother, and that whatever is deemed appropriate by the Father will come about. Even though you may stand and continue to watch your brother as he flounders about—and you may wrench your hands and embrace him over and over again—know deep within that all is well, that nothing that is helpful to your brother is withheld, and that you may always look beyond the mask and have—and rejoice in—another holy embrace—and thus know the Father expressed as your brother, and know that this is knowing the Supreme Deity. For the Supreme Deity is expressed in the peace that comes upon you; and the love that wells up within your heart, as well as the love that you receive from your brother, is expressed in the Pure and Holy Light you see in his heart as you gently part the clouds that stand before it and gaze deep within—and become so engrossed in that gaze that you no longer think of your brother as anything but holy.

This I would have you do. And remember, for some brothers the best way of helping them in that moment might be just a kind deed, a smile, or, for someone who is performing a menial task, just sharing of the earthly means of exchange (the money you may have in your wallet) and just simply saying to a brother who is going through his own process of needing to learn to see the Father in others—just speak to this one in need softly and say—"The Father has laid upon my heart to deliver this gift to you; it is a great blessing for me to have been chosen to do this, and it is with great joy that I do it; and please, don't thank me, thank the Father, for it was His prompting, and it was his Gift—It is He who put it in my wallet, just for you, and protected it there until the opportunity came so that I might be the vessel who delivered it to you." And if there is a chore a brother is doing, you might say, "Allow me to lift this for you, to help you, to take care of some of these many chores you have, so that you may finish your tasks more quickly and have a moment of peace and quiet in which you might then bask in stillness in the Father's Love."

Remember, I do walk the earth, and I also am in your heart. I can express through you, and if you allow Me to do this, you may one day even have a brother say to you, "I recognize Jesus, the one we call the Christ—I recognize Him in you. How nice that you came to me today, that you allowed Him to come in you." And so, my dear ones, this is My message for you today: Remember your brothers. That is why you are here. Remember, you have the same mission I had and still have. What greater joy, what greater creativity, could you have? For creativity is extending the Father's Love, His Light, His Joy, His Energy, and when you allow it to be done through you, and touch a brother's heart and bring him back into the fold, you have actually done a double deed of creation. The Father delights in those who desire to do so, and certainly you know that I delight in you. Wherever you are and you ask for Me, I come. You may know Me sitting beside you as you drive your car. You may know Me walking beside you on the street. You may know Me within you as you go about your daily tasks. And when you say, "Help me. I don't know what is the best thing to be done." Then relax a moment and allow Me—allow that knowing—to well up within you, and suddenly you will know what your mission is in that moment. Then you will smile, and there will be a radiance about you as you realize that you have in that moment, in that deed, allowed yourself to be the Father expressed on earth as one of His children. Go forth in Peace, knowing you are always cared for. I bless you now and always, forevermore.

MESSAGE ABOUT COMMUNION

MESSAGE ABOUT COMMUNION

Would the Blessed Father speak to us of communion, tell us what it is, what really happens when we commune?

*As you come before Me in great love and joy, in appreciation for That which you recognize as being Myself, and as you feel That welling up within your own heart, you recognize that It is identical with what you come before Me to know and to experience. And in doing so, the spirit within you merges with That which you recognize as Me, and in the merging you realize that It was never apart, It was never separate—It was always one. And the communion itself is only a recognition of what always was and always will be, which **is** into all eternity—a state in which there can be no separation, for separation itself is only an imagination that has gone awry. It is an idea, conceived within the mind, to be that which cannot be, to be apart from, simply as a way of letting the imagination* *go in directions that are not real—allowing it to fantasize about something that could not be. And it was this fantasy that brought about what you have sometimes called "the Fall"—an imagination that allowed you to think of yourself as being separate and to think of yourself as doing and creating in your own way, but in a way that was not in accordance with My Will. It was not a way that had its roots in oneness and in extending, but rather a way that was trying to create something that was not a part of you—an attempt to allow yourself to, as it were, paint a picture and let it have its own existence, and that which you imagined and attempted to create very quickly, in its limited state of awareness, forgot its origin.*

*As a result of the forgetting, there came about feelings of fear, of insecurity—feelings of a need to defend oneself—and as this fantasy became the place where your thoughts dwelt, your mind appeared to be confined; and it became a habit for you. You forgot your source; you forgot where you came from; you forgot where you actually really are, because it was as if you had opened a window and looked outside, and then in perceiving yourself as being out **there**, you forgot that* *you were still inside the room. And as your experience of these aberrations, these fantasies that appeared to be real, became so gruesome, so fearful, you called for help. You asked to be allowed to return, which in reality was not a proper request because you had never left, but actually you were asking to be helped to release the fantasies and be freed from them (to withdraw from the window, to turn away from it), and to look back into the Heart whence you came—to gaze upon the Beauty and the Light there (the Purity), to know the Love that surrounded you (the Love in which you dwelt and existed), and to know that Joy again.*

And then came the concept of communing, which for you came to mean, in the beginning, shorter periods of time in which you turned back and gazed into that Light. Then you returned again into the world you thought you had created—where your seeming existence appeared to be, and where you saw others who appeared to be lost in the fantasy. And so you began to describe this period of gazing back into the Light as a period of communing, which was really just a recognition of where you always were—where you still are. This was a short period of forgetting your fantasies before you returned, *realizing that now you had a new mission, you had a task, you had an obligation—you had an **opportunity**—to go back into the fantasized world that seemed separate, and gather unto you and speak to those who were still lost in that fantasy—speak to them of this wonderful experience of returning to knowledge, to knowing, to living in the true reality of what you are, as well as speak to and encourage them to allow you to take them by the hand—to put your arm around them and bring them back into this experience of what would, at first, seem to them to be a fantasy, until they realized it was true reality.*

And as you brought them back, you said, "Oh, Blessed Father, I bring one with me who was lost—lost in his fantasies—and who thought there was no hope. I bring this one with me and I say, 'Help him that he may (in the beginning—for a moment at least) release those fantasies, gaze into the Light, vanish into the Love, know whence he came, and know the security of belonging in You—of knowing that he is there with You—so that he may then, after knowing this, release his fear and feelings of insecurity, and at least for a short while just rest in that knowing of eternal limitless Joy, and limitless

Light and Love.' And then may he return with me to go back into that world of fantasy seeking others—some who are crying out, who desire to return, and who will agree to come quickly, but also going further and recognizing those who have never called out, who have never thought there was a hope, and who seem to have lost all will and dwell in a stupor—in the sense of being stunned, gazing into nothingness, and feeling there is no hope. May he touch such a one upon the shoulder, greet him in love, and say to him, 'My dear brother, I come to embrace you; I come to speak to you of love, of joy; I come to lead you away from this grayness in which you dwell—a murky darkness that seems to zap you of all feelings of any sort of existence, of energy, of any light or hope, of any love. First of all, allow me to just embrace you, to fold you into my arms, to let you know how much you are loved and what a joy it is that I have found you in this land of nothingness, and then to gaze upon your countenance, to speak to you of the untold beauty that is there within your heart waiting for me to gently part clouds away—to remove them as you allow—in order that I may gasp at the beauty of a Light of breathtaking brilliance, and be transported by the Love that is there waiting to be joined with, so that you may know that this is what communion is: a joining—a joining of two like beings.

"'And in so joining you allow me to take you back with me into the full knowing and experience of this limitless Love and Joy, so that you may know total communion with the Father and know that you rest in His Heart with me, and we may—at least for a short while before returning into that darkness to seek another—forget the darkness, knowing that it does not exist. It never existed—it was just a wild fantasy, a fantasy that can be released, for it was based upon nothing. It was based upon a desire to think of, to know of, ourselves as being separate, which we really are not, and now we want to allow that fantasy to disappear.'" This, My child, is what communion is—a returning into a knowing of that which always was. And I am pleased that you want to know more about it—about your role in assisting your brothers.

With respect to the fantasy, please comment on the role of the Son and the creation of the physical universe.

NOTE: The Son referred to in the answer given below is not the third Person of the Trinity, or Jesus, but rather the Sonship—all created souls who are considered to be one Son, with Jesus being the first embodiment of the *whole* Son.

First of all, I would speak to you of true creation. Creation came about when I, in My own Heart and Mind, desired to create a Son, One so like unto Myself that no difference could be seen except that I extended the Son so that I could behold Him and know of Myself—know of My own Being—as I saw My Son there extending and radiating this limitless Light and this Love—extending great waves of It that had no end. This was true creation—an extension that was not apart from or separated from Myself. I had great joy in this Son—as I looked upon Him, My joy had no end. And I encouraged My Son to also create in the same way: to extend parts of Himself in great Love and behold that, and yet to know that it was also Myself—it was not an extension only of the Son, but an extension of Myself, knowing Itself, all mingled and swirled together and just radiating Love with great joy.

And yet, the Son desired also something called "free will." In My limitless Love, I allowed what was called free will, and yet it was itself not a total creation—it only appeared to be—for in free will there was total free will, and there was the ability to imagine that one could have a will of one's own that might be separate from the Father. But the Son was not separate from the Father; therefore, such a free will was not really true—it was a fantasy. And in this free will the Son went forth rejoicing in Its creative processes, but, as it might appear (or as a storyteller might say), one bright and beautiful day the thought came into the mind of the Son, "In My free will I could be separate from the Father and go about just doing my own thing. I could create all these things in My own way." And so, the fantasy continued, and the Son began what might be called by some on earth the creation of the great physical and manifest universe—the fantasies. This was not a true creation—it was an imaginary creation, and this imaginary creation was born in this imaginary free will of the Son. And yet, the Son had great Power, great Energy, and did in a burst (in this imaginary world) bring about what has been thought of as the creation of the Father.

Although the forms that were created were imaginary, they were still created within the Son, who was within the Father, and there is nothing in this manifest, created, physical world (or universe) that is not a part of the Father. So, in the great burst of Energy and Light, as it might be beheld on a physical level, and the Love that would be perceived and thought of as separate and limited, there (always lying underneath) was the Father. This world could not have existed if the Father had not also been there indwelling it and waiting for those identifying themselves with the perceived forms to come to recognition that only the forms were a fantasy, but the true reality was still the Father (connected with the Father)— always with the Father and having the ability with Its will, Its fantasized free will, to return to the recognition of what always was and could never be changed. And so, what appeared to have been a great physical burst of Light and Love in the creation of the universe (that was separate and a world of separate beings)—what appeared to be such—was just a fantasy, and at any point in time any being which appears to be lost in this world has its perceived free will to turn and say, "Take me back. I would know my Father." And in so doing, it returns "of its own free will," as you would have it, to knowing that it still rests in Me. I have unlimited Joy in My Son and unconditional Love for Him, and I have never condemned Him of His fantasies that went awry and appeared to cause Him to suffer.

I always knew that the suffering He thought He was experiencing would lead Him back, rushing into My arms and saying, "I thank you, Father, for what You are and for what I am, and for bringing Me to the recognition of it—and now for allowing me to assist in bringing all others who have thought they were lost into this recognition, so that their perceived ideas may just simply fall away, as if they have lifted a robe from their shoulders and allowed it to drop." And you know you rest in My arms, in My heart; and your joy is full. This, My Son, explains to you this great fantasy of nothingness that you may at any point release.

The Heavenly Father is asked to tell us how to commune with Him, or what we must do in order to allow communion to take place.

The first step in communion is to desire it, but there is also a precursor to the desire, for many: it is to become so lost in the fantasy that you begin to feel that you suffer; and there is pain, there is agony; and you want to know Love, you want to feel Love, you cry out for Love. And as you cry out for Love, then you desire to know it—you open your heart (to some extent) to the possibility, and as you desire it and ask for it, then everything that is needed in this process—of allowing the scales to be removed from your eyes and you to know that you stand in Holy Light—will be prepared for you. You then desire to know Perfection and Holiness, and to release all your fantasies of other than that so that they may be removed. But one of the ways in which you are assisted in this process is to look upon another brother, and as you at first see the form, see the limited nature, and also become aware of his feelings of hopelessness (his agony, and his pain)—as you understand that and identify with it to some extent—then agree to consider this form, these limitations, to be just a very thin mask across Holiness—and agree to reach forth and say, "Allow me to part those clouds gently so that I may gaze upon the purity which you are." And as you gaze upon it, that within you that is identical with it wells up within your heart, *and you feel the communing—you feel a joining of yourself with this brother—because what he is, is so beautiful, and you have allowed the mask to be drawn away (the veil of nothingness). And as you see that—allow yourself to be willing to desire to see that—you allow the mask and veil across your own heart to fall, for they fall simultaneously. And you feel that within yourself; you embrace your brother; and then you know this oneness that **is**. This is how you begin to know communion.*

As you do this more often, you will then realize that you can also just, at any moment, release all your fantasies and allow that communion with Me to take place, but it is much easier to begin by looking for it in your brothers and participating in drawing back the veil, for as you become a part of the process of your brother, you know indescribable love; you realize your oneness with him; and you then realize that participating in that process of your brother is a part of your own process of returning to full knowingness, for you cannot be apart from him, and to know him fully as yourself, you must also join in his process. This, My child, is the process of communing.

Are there different ways of communing?

*Surely, as you recognize that each brother is unique in some way, and each brother has his own preferences and appearances of talents and gifts, you will come to know that, for some, one way might be easier than another. For some, to understand intellectually the process of this fantasized creation and the process of returning by lifting the veil, by desiring to return—desiring to gaze upon the Holiness in a brother—for some, the intellectual process is the easiest way, for the world of ideas is the world in which they, in their limited state, like to dwell—in which they have joy. Then for others, it is the heart, the love—they desire to understand how to draw that veil back gently and, by using the imagination, fantasize initially that there is this limitless Love of the Father in the heart of a brother, and as they draw the veil back, to imagine: it is the Father there!—and they then **know** it in this Love and this limitless state. They then commune: first, by using their imagination and their fantasy to change what was a dream—a dream of pain and suffering, and guilt and fear—*

to a dream of no guilt and no pain—by fantasizing pure and holy Light, and eternal Love, in that heart.

This is a process, and yet, you may also at any moment just simply pause and say, "Father, I know that I am your child. In this moment I want to know myself resting in Your Heart— to experience this limitless Love—so that it may be refreshed in my memory and I may be better able to go back into the world of fantasy that went awry and bring it into the experience and knowledge of my brothers." So, for each one there is prepared a way—the easiest way possible for him or her—and they will be assisted. They need only have the willingness and the desire—or even at some point say, "My desire and willingness are weak; grant me the desire and willingness to know this." Even that is of great benefit to your brothers.

What is the place of communion in creation? What is its purpose?

In the original creation of extension of My beloved Son, communion, you might say, was constant—never ending—for extension is not separation, and so communion might be said to be eternal—without end. The place of communion in the created worlds (that were the result of that fantasy) is that it is the process of returning to full knowledge and experience of resting in the Father, and knowing that you are His Son and never have been apart from Him—nor could you be. In the world of fantasy, communion exists, in the beginning, as a series of experiences, steps along the way—going from one experience of communion to another and broadening your understanding, broadening your view and your experience of reality. At first the experience of reality is a perception, but it becomes a knowing of true creation, which can only be in oneness—which is in the Father, for true creation is not in existence apart from Him.

Is there anything more that can be added about how to commune with the Divine Spirit in other people?

Communion always begins with a desire, and in some cases it may come about because of your perceptions in this world of fantasy that went awry. It may be a desire to see something other than the pain, the ugliness, the separation, the agony, that you are perceiving with your physical senses. You are weary of this and you desire to commune because you want to see something better, and in the beginning this may be, more often than not, the reason that you would desire to do so. But, My dear child, as you do this more and more often, you will desire to commune, not to get away from these things, but in order to know once again that wholeness, that oneness, and to know your brother as whole and at-one with Myself and with you. It will be a desire to know beauty and joy and wholeness, and to release a perception of anything other than that—even the perception of perfection—so that you may go beyond it and know the joy that satisfies any kind of longing or yearning; know the love that releases any kind of feeling of fear, of insecurity, of being alone; and know that you rest always in My Heart. And as you begin to desire communion for this reason, you will do it more and more and more, until one day you will realize that you actually are dwelling in this state constantly, and those perceived forms and that fantasy— that fantasy of horror (the awful movie you allowed yourself to make)—was just nothing.

As you encounter your brothers who may seem to be lost in that movie (the fantasy), you are so anchored in My Love, and in the vision of Holiness, that you hardly perceive what your brother is seeing, feeling, and thinking that he knows. You gaze with such intensity upon My Being in his heart that it awakens him, and he realizes that this fantasy of his is not real. You touch that within him, and as he looks upon you, he thinks he is seeing something within you that is a fantasy, but one that is beautiful; and it is because you have embraced the spirit within him that you bring it forth to his remembrance—a remembrance that is never lost, but, of his own doing and his own will, it would be extremely difficult for him to recall. But by your focusing upon it so that you see nothing else—this holiness within his heart—you allow that remembrance to come forth with such ease that he is amazed by it, he looks upon it, and he is drawn towards it and wants to enter into it. Then he says, "Take me with you. Never release me. I want to be with you." And you, in your great love, put your arms around him and feel yourself merge with him; and you know this oneness, this being in holiness, this perceived communion that really never ceases to exist.

Is communing then the best way to do our part in helping to dispel sorrow and suffering in the world, and in bringing hope and joy to others?

*Absolutely, **absolutely**! But, My dear child, this does not in any way mean that you just get yourself blissed out in this communion and forget that, for some of your brothers, they are not in that state totally with you. As you desire to know this in fullness, you also have such great desire to assist in helping your brothers regain this memory, that you would never leave one stranded there in the darkness crying out. And you realize that you must at first meet them where they are and realize that, for some, the first step in helping them could just be a kind deed: a smile that radiates love at a time when they are perhaps being a bit unkind to you, or being helpful and kind with infinite patience—patience that never accepts the dream of fantasy as true and that does not belittle them by reacting to it, but looks straight through their fantasy and acknowledges that they are pure and holy, that they are your brothers, and that what they perceive in no way belittles them or causes you to feel that they have any less value to you or to Me. You meet them where they are, and you grant them* *every kind and loving deed that helps and assists them in their return, for you are eternally interlocked with each one—intertwined with them—and assist in their returning. And you also realize that this **is** your greatest joy, for you could not know your joy apart from them.*

Does this then answer the question of whether there is more we should do after communing, or how we can best be vessels for the Father to help our brothers and sisters?

Yes, communion itself, in the beginning (for you), is awakening that memory, and then after it is awakened, you realize your role in this process—your role in assisting—and communion eventually becomes a constant thing.

Why is there a reluctance to commune at times?

For some brothers, and at times for yourself (as you so well know), My dear child, the reluctance comes because of your allowing yourself to identify with this world of form and fantasy—to identify with this perceived separation (this perceived free will to be separated from Me). And then as you look upon your brothers, you see the same thing that you have fantasized yourself, and you reject it because you reject your own perceptions (for you see that they are not full, they are not pure, they are not holy—that they are limited, they are sick). As you see that in your brother and you reject it, you are then reluctant. You may say, "This one is so obnoxious. Why would I want to see the Father in him?" And so you are reluctant. It takes great desire and will on your part to get over this hump, and it only takes a couple of experiences of just looking beyond for you, after an initial rejection, to realize that you are not happy in your condemnation, and that your joy is to commune. And you assist your brothers in also getting over this hump by doing such with them, for as you know, many times have you gone deep within and talked to your brothers, embraced them, spoken to them of the great love within them, and even asked that they allow Me within them to bless you. And then after such a communing you have come to know, to realize, that it assisted your brothers in releasing some of their fantasies, some of their pain.

So, there is resistance, and in part this is because of having so allowed yourself to get lost in the fantasy, but also, as you *begin to return and desire to assist your brothers, this resistance serves a holy purpose, for it allows you to understand your brothers. It also allows **them** to realize that you understand, for they then see that you can also sometimes reject—the difference being that you use it as a tool and go beyond it. And as they see that you do that, they desire to do so themselves. So, the resistance (at some point, as you desire and ask for all things in your experience to be holy) becomes a holy tool in your process of returning, and in your process of being a part of the return of your brothers.*

Is there an incongruity between some of the messages about creation that seem to indicate all creation was of God and other messages that seem to indicate that creation of the physical universe came about through the Son?

This has also been addressed earlier in this session. Those who come seeking the process of the heart, seek to know from the heart of Love, and in the beginning they still lean heavily upon teachings from the past. Initially, teachings are given in the way in which they can best accept, for so are they best assisted. Some teachings have taught of the creation as being totally by the Father, and so, this is not challenged at first. But in this session We have also spoken of these things, and there is no incongruity—it is just that there is a difference in perception as one journeys along the way.

A message from the Supreme Being is requested.

*And so, now, My dear child, be assured that you rest in My Heart—you are always in My Heart. You participate in this process with your brothers, but you always know that you are in My Heart—even when you are in the created worlds. I created you just simply to know Myself extended so that I could gaze upon It, not as a separate child or being, but that I might know **Myself**—and My Light and My Love that radiate, for these are expressions of My Being—which, without the Child, was a state of total serenity and stillness—a state of being. It is always My great delight to create and know My Creation, to look upon the Beauty and Holiness of It, and to see Myself—to see Myself there. And now, I urge you: give up all personal desires—all fantasies—and allow yourself to be Myself coming into the experience of your brothers, who are lost in their dream—in their fantasy. Allow Me to lead you to* *each experience—to lead you moment by moment without any resistance on your part—without a desire to go to a particular place, be with a particular person, or have certain circumstances or situations. Allow your greatest desire to be to allow Me to come to your brothers as you and allow Me, in My infinite Wisdom, to know which brothers are now ready for a helping hand—and in what way. Allow me to lead you to each one. Greet each one as Myself come to you, realizing that in their perceived state of separation they feel lost, and your helping hand is the greatest thing that you could allow. Realize that it is your duty, your obligation, to assist your brothers, for you know that, in drawing back that veil and looking upon Myself in them, you are fulfilled.*

*So, go forth from this day forward, asking all through the day, "Father, What is Your Will in this moment? Lead me where You would have me go; help me to always recognize You; help me not to be deceived by the mask, the veil, across the heart of my brother." And know that in desiring this, all is perfect; all is arranged; all is provided for. Depend upon Me. Trust me totally, even as your Blessed Brother, known as Jesus, the Christ, trusted me totally—He **never** doubted! He is* *your example. Follow Him. And know He walks beside you—He is always there! And now you know what your calling is, what your job is (your task), but consider it to be an **opportunity**, a **blessing** from the Father. Go forth each moment of the day desiring to allow My Light and Love to radiate from you, to embrace your brothers in spirit, as well as in body when it is appropriate. Embrace them all, and release all concerns about your health, nutrition, your finances, what is needed, all provisions for the journey—give that over to Me and walk forth free, for only when you are totally free can you be, as an empty vessel, of most assistance to your brothers—and allow Me to manifest and express as you on earth.*

MESSAGE ABOUT FORGIVENESS

MESSAGE ABOUT FORGIVENESS

The Heavenly Father is asked to please define what forgiveness is—tell us what it entails.

As you seek to know Me, to approach Me in spirit, initially you may find that you are not able to do so because there are memories, perceptions, that block your view. And these memories and perceptions involve your brothers. They involve judgments you have made out of a sense of insecurity, a sense of lack, and in an attitude that is lacking in unconditional love. Forgiveness is when you allow these images, these perceptions, these judgments, to dissolve; and as you seek to commune with Me, forgiveness is the most important technique you can use. For as you seek to know My Presence, it is easier for you to seek to discover that Presence of My Spirit in your brothers, and at first, there appears to be a veil across the heart of your brother so that you do not see that Spirit of Mine there. And yet, my child, it is your judgments that have caused this seeming state of separation and isolation—what might also be labeled as a sense of exile from the Father. Forgiveness is in allowing those things to disappear, but forgiveness is more than the traditional definition of the word, which implies simply to excuse a shortcoming of your brothers, although you still cling to the memory of it. Forgiveness in the true sense of the word is releasing all those judgments, and you may do so simply by observing your judgments and then agreeing—allowing yourself, that is—to make a different judgment, to choose a different perception— one that is more loving, one that entails accepting a sense of perfection in your brother.

So, at first you observe your perceptions and your judgments of that which is unholy. Then you choose a holy judgment, a holy perception, a holy image; and even though you may think of this as also an illusion, it is a step towards releasing those unholy judgments. For in agreeing to consider that your brother might be a part of Myself, pure and holy, lacking in nothing, you then allow the door to be opened so that you may truly look through the image; for the holy image, the holy judgment, itself is so thin that you very easily are able to pass through it and gaze upon that which is Myself, waiting for your embrace. And in doing so—in accepting this embrace, accepting this holiness—then you allow yourself to release all those misinterpretations that have caused you to feel inadequate, to feel vulnerable, to feel lost, and to feel lack. So, My dear child, forgiveness is releasing your judgments of that which is not pure and whole in exchange for another judgment, another image—that of purity and holiness—for this is the key that leads you on to communion.

How does forgiveness fit in with plan of salvation? Why is it needed?

Forgiveness is needed because those judgments you have made of your brother are blocks that prevent you from seeing that which he truly is, and as long as you cling to these judgments, these misperceptions, these nightmarish dreams—the mask you think you see before your brother's heart—as long as you cling to these, you cannot know the truth—you will not commune with Me. And your salvation is to have these things melt away so that you instead cling to Me, so that you rush into My arms, and you also accept that I am in your brother's heart, for he is a part of Me—I laid a part of My Heart in his. And until you agree to commune with Me in your brother's heart, you need salvation, you still are in a state of seeming exile. Forgiveness is a gift, a gift that I have prepared for you as a way of effecting your salvation and allowing you to release all those misperceptions and judgments you have of yourself, as well as your brothers.

Is there anything further to be said concerning the efficacy of forgiveness?

Without forgiveness you remain lost in a world of darkness, a world in which you perceive your brothers as attacking you. You feel you must seek safety, and you know not where to turn. Forgiveness has the effect of allowing all of this to disappear. It is the greatest technique that could be given to you in order to release you; and although, in the beginning, you may feel resistant to using this, consider, my child: when you turn to Me and ask for help, I would only give you that which is best. As a loving Father, the Source of your own being, I would only give you that which is of most effectiveness, and that which is easiest for you. And even when your willingness to accept and to make use of this gift of Mine is weak, you need only ask Me to help you to have that willingness. Then you will see opportunities come in which you will be willing, and it will be very easy for you. And those opportunities that might be more of a challenge will be reserved for later when you have become accustomed to allowing yourself to release those things—and also accustomed to the experience of Holiness, of Beauty, of Pure and Holy Light, of indescribable Love (and you trust that this is what awaits you)—and when you have that willingness to do so.

Concerning those challenges to our willingness, what are the obstacles we as humans encounter in forgiving—what is our resistance?

When you look upon the world about you with your physical eyes—when you perceive the world with all of your physical senses—then it appears to you that there is no other way of perceiving it—that this is all you can see—and you see a world of beings who are totally separate, each competing with the other—often with an intent to harm (to try to use the other to benefit from, and leave the other with less). And looking upon the world with these physical senses—observing all of the violence and the hate in the world around you—you sense the greatest obstacle to forgiveness, but you must accept, My child, to seek to know what is true, and to accept that Truth is Spirit. To know and experience this you must do so with the spirit within yourself. And you must accept to withdraw your attention from the physical senses and perceptions, and from the desires of the physical world, so that you can then experience with the spirit within you, know the spirit within your brothers, and come to know that what the physical senses convey to you is a misinterpretation, and has caused you to feel lost and abandoned—and without love. You release these things, and as you begin to experience with your spirit—that Spirit of Mine within you—then you lose your fear of all those images, all those seeming threats, and the fear of lack and being alone.

Is there anything more the Heavenly Father would tell us about how to accomplish forgiveness?

In the beginning, forgiveness is an incident, and as time goes on it appears to be isolated incidents that you may, at first, suspect to be only a dream, an illusion, but if you desire to know Me and the truth of your brothers, you will continue and be diligent in your pursuit of those incidents, which become more and more frequent as you apply yourself to do this, and become more and more convincing until a point is reached where you begin to suspect that the world you perceive with your physical senses is the one that is an illusion—is the one whose reality is suspect. And you will also realize that the world of the senses has never brought you joy, has never brought you peace—a peace of resting in a spirit of knowingness that there is only Love and only Joy.

Are there methods or techniques that would assist us in forgiving?

The method most effective is to consider that what you perceive with your earthly senses could be a dream or a story—a tale that is spun out of the imagination—and being such, it can be changed because you can imagine differently—you can choose to spin a different tale, to tell a different story. And so, as some brother you encounter causes a reaction within you, you reject him, and as you have thoughts of unkindness towards him, just stop and think about it—find a place of quiet (this is needed in the beginning). And then you decide: "Let me tell a beautiful story about this brother. I am going to make up a tale that is so beautiful! I am going to change this brother into a child of light and love—a child of God." And tell yourself, "In his heart is all the beauty one could ever expect to experience. This child came to me this day, and he was wearing a mask, a rather unkindly mask—a mask that showed him as attacking me. And at first, I mistook the mask for reality, but now in the story I am telling about my brother, the mask was just a ruse—it was a game he was playing with me—and he fooled me with it. But behind that mask is holiness, there is purity; and so, in this moment I approach my brother, and say, 'You were teasing me today. You fooled me at first, but now I see through it all. I come to you in great love, and I desire that you allow me to embrace you and to gently lift the mask away so that I may gaze upon that which you truly are, that I may allow **you** to embrace **me** and awaken the true being within me so that my own mask may fall away and the two of us merge in a dance of love and *of joy—that we may sing praises to our Father that in this moment we have experienced the true reality of what we are.'"*

And so, My child, once you agree to do this (although it may be somewhat with an unwillingness), once you agree to do this, you will find the experience waiting for you, and the memory will remain with you. And at some point you will desire to try this again, for it was so beautiful that it released you from all your anxieties, all your sorrows, and all your feelings of imperfection. Then you come back again when you seek another brother, and you say, "I want to do this once again. I want to know what is really there and release those other things."

As you begin to do this, you have these isolated experiences. And yet, sometimes you may have misgivings, for as you go forth into the world, all this seems to recede into the back of your mind, and all the perceptions with the body senses are so up-front—they are in your face and you are seeing them— and all of a sudden you have condemned another brother. And then you may feel a little bit guilty about that, but another technique is this: instead of feeling guilty, you say, "This is just a reminder to me! Now I know. I should not condemn myself for these negative feelings I had. I should just consider that this is what was necessary to remind me; otherwise, if things seemed to be going so smoothly, I would forget to look beyond the mask. But when I see a little ugliness, I remember, 'Oh, I want to see something else.'" And so, now, another technique is to always interpret those experiences as reminders, and also opportunities—opportunities that bring blessings to you, and also to your brothers, for every embrace of the holiness in another brother causes more thickness in the veil before his heart and your own to fall away, and that veil becomes thinner and thinner, and brings about the salvation of your brother and of yourself.

And then, there are other techniques: remember, my child, every day to come to Me and say, "Remind me each day, Father, more and more often than ever before that you are in the heart of a brother, and even though I am involved in all the activities of life, place this thought into my mind so that I may, in just an instant (for a few seconds), think, 'There is holiness behind all of this I am perceiving. There is the Father there waiting for me.' Remind me, Father, to do this, and I set my intention this day to find You, to discover You, behind the masks that parade back and forth in front of me." And do bear in mind, My child, that the intention you set has great power to it. The intention you deliberately set for your day has great bearing upon what happens, upon how you interpret the day (the events of the day) and upon how you allow yourself to either experience happiness, or to be fooled by the clouds and masks you may see, and then allow yourself to be depressed and lacking in joy.

So, remember these techniques, and remember, when someone is really getting on your nerves—someone is causing you to put up barriers, and you begin to sense this feeling of rejection—remember: this is just a reminder; this is knocking on the door of your heart. It is a call to you: look deeper, go beyond the mask, focus your attention upon this—have the intention to so focus upon it that all else melts away. And you may then know yourself resting in My arms, carried forth by Me in Love and Joy—and with My abundance poured forth upon you—so that there is no experience of lack, but only one of joy, only dancing in the Light, only singing with your brothers songs of thankfulness and gratitude to the Father that His plan is perfect—that He has provided a way out of every wayward glance or intention, out of every detour you have decided to take for yourself, so that you may find your way back. And in the experience of doing so, you may understand your brothers, understand how they feel (where they are) and understand how to help them to join with you, arm in arm, coming before Me in great love and asking, "Father, today I have no intentions of my own. I desire to do Your Will. What is Your assignment for this day? Lead me to it, for I desire that each brother know the joy I have—and the Love you extend always without limits."

How can others be encouraged to seek to forgive?

For many, the beginning of such encouragement could be telling them of your own experiences. And for that reason you have been encouraged to do so—speaking to them, sharing the stories of your experiences with other brothers, and also sharing with them the stories of your thoughts of feeling deprived, lonely, and lost—of being abandoned—and how you yourself came to release those things. Ask each day that, as you encounter your brothers, the Father may provide the opportunity for you to share these things, for this is also a part of what you might call "the puzzle being completed." Looking upon the heart of your brothers is surely the big step, but you also hasten their journey of return by such things as telling them stories—writing these stories down, sharing them—for as your brothers hear of these things, they will also desire to come to know of them, and as they desire and ask for this, then come the opportunities to share with them the techniques of accomplishing (bringing about) forgiveness. And as you share the stories of forgiveness you have offered and the benefits of such—the communing that came about as a result—then you awaken in them even more a desire to do this.

But forget not, there are many other ways: as you go about your daily tasks, you can release your brothers in your heart and in your mind. You may not even say a word to them, or you may gently touch someone on the shoulder; you may offer a kind word or just a treat (a snack)—a kindness of some kind that is a token, a symbol, of your appreciation of the purity that is within their hearts. And be not deceived: some of your brothers may have a veil across their eyes and not see truly, but they will surely recognize how you feel about them; and when you accept the holiness within them, it is not possible that this could be disguised and they would not be able to sense it—and then appreciate your own appreciation of them.

And they will come to you to experience that radiation of Light and Love, which is Myself in your heart that you have simply allowed full sway; that is, you have allowed the door to your heart to open and all veils to fall away. Then the sun of My Light—the sunshine of My Being—beams forth upon them, and they will feel refreshed and also feel a sense of love welling up within them as a response to your own love. Just ask each day that I provide the opportunities and help you to recognize when one of these techniques is appropriate, so that you pause a moment and allow Me, through you, to bless your brothers.

Is there a message from Jesus?

Blessed brothers and sisters of earth, I come extending my arms to you, beckoning to you, and saying, Come unto Me, for I am with you, even as I was on the earth two thousand years ago. You need only call My Name, you need only call for help, and I will surely be with you. And if you allow yourself to believe it, you can sense, you can feel, My Presence, which is the Presence of an Elder Brother who comes in the name of the Father—the Father of Love, the Father of Holiness. You can know the Presence of an Elder Brother who comes to you to embrace you, so that you may feel that you are not alone, that you are secure, and that as you go forth into the world, there is always a Companion—One walking beside you, One speaking with you, One who listens to you, One who is always ready to hear of the problems you have encountered (your difficulties), and also One who will whisper to you in spirit and give you ideas—Holy Ideas from the Father That will help you to embrace the world and respond as a child of God.

I am always there; I never leave you. But it is to your advantage sometimes to consciously ask for Me so that you may then more easily trust that I am there, for surely you do believe that My Promises are true, that I have never failed you—even though you perhaps are not aware of it, I have never failed you—and I was always there. I walk with you through every experience, and I protect you. There is no world of chance when you rely upon Me, for I come representing the Father, exemplifying Him to you—simply in a way that you might more easily accept. I walk with you, and when you ask for this, there are no mishaps in your life, there are no accidents. I encourage you. Whatever might come up, that might seem to you to be "all hell breaking loose," is an opportunity, and it is not only an opportunity for you to look beyond the mask, it is an opportunity for you to allow Me to be in you and to touch another brother—to reach forth in spirit and gently touch that heart in love, as you reach forth with your hands and touch them. And as they are unloading their anger upon you, you may gently smile, look upon the heart in love and say, "Blessed Jesus, Holy Brother, be in me; touch them; bring peace to their hearts; bring an experience of love—may this be the event that causes them to turn back towards the Light."

Always accept that every event that comes, no matter how traumatic or how nerve-racking it may be, can be the door that opens the way for your brother. And you can be the vessel which turns his gaze backwards, turns him looking towards the Light. You may speak to him and say, "Look intensely and deeply, for as you look through the clouds, you will see that which will draw you easily, further and further. For once you have a glimpse, you are reminded of that which you had long since forgotten, which you don't so easily forget now. This experience is a blessing, and We give thanks for it."

He speaks to the vessel.

Go forth, my child, allowing Me to be in your heart, for I am the Father, come to you. I am the Father in your heart. You and I are one, and we are also one with the Father, for we have no existence apart from Him. All those things that you have perceived as being separate were just a fantasy (a fantasy you allowed yourself to take seriously), and now you release it and say, "What a bad bedtime story that was! Now, let's have a good one—a beautiful story! Let's talk about the Father and our holy brothers, and journey back towards the Light. And as we encounter each form, we gently release it, gently brush it aside and gaze into that pure and holy light it was trying to obscure, it was trying to hide. We allow that Light now to shine without hindrance. And we walk forth journeying towards the Light, gathering unto us all those we encounter—even those who may seem to have no interest. As we touch them gently, they will smile, and they will then feel drawn to join us as we go back."

I bless you; I bless you with My Love. I give you My embrace, and I thank you that you have accepted to be an empty vessel, for every empty vessel who joins with Me makes the way for your brothers, who are wandering in darkness, easier than it was before, for more and more vessels walk in the murky darkness and cause the mist to rise and the Light to be known—to be seen—and the Love experienced. We go forth together—I in your heart. You allow yourself to be Me, and we bless the world simply through acknowledgment of that which truly is—acknowledgment of the Truth—acknowledgment of the Father and that there is no brother who is not pure and holy—admirable—one in whom a glimpse of the Light in his heart causes us to rejoice. I thank you that you allow this, and We go forth together.

MESSAGE ABOUT CREATION

MESSAGE ABOUT CREATION

NOTE: The reader is referred back to the second question and answer in "Message about Communing" for introductory information about creation.

There are teachings that free will was the "first distortion;" the Logos, also known as Creative Principle or Love was the "second distortion;" and Light was the "third distortion." Why are these called distortions, and were they caused by the desire of the children of God to be separate from Him?

As I desired to create a child, known by you as the Son, created as a part of Myself and not as a separate being, the child also had the ability to create—to continue creating as I did—and had great joy in that. After some time, as it would appear, the child did have a strange idea come into its mind—a question: "How would it be to create that which is separate? How would it be to myself be separate from the Father and then do my own creations as it might please me?" And as soon as this idea came into the mind of the Son, it caused the appearance of the first illusion: an illusion of a free will that was not anchored in the Father—a free will that was not bound by the Father's way of creating—and that could choose its own way. But this free will was only a fantasy because the Son of God, being a part of God, could have no will separate from that of the Father, and this fantasy was the result of the illusion that one might be separate; and yet, it was a pretension—it was the imagination gone wild. It was not pure, and it was not holy, and even though the Son had chosen (at least temporarily) to journey down this road that would lead to much pain and suffering, it really was all just make-believe; it was all in the mind—just a fantasy.

And yet the Son had not totally forgotten its Source at that point, as it would seem, and still at times glanced backwards—back to the Source whence it came—and perceived the Father as being an incredibly beautiful and blinding Light, Pure and Holy, beckoning to it, and also a Love that had no limits—a Love that always said, "I regard not your misconceptions, your fantasies—this aberration of creation of *yours—for it is not true, and I welcome you back into the knowledge of that which you are." And so, my child, understand that when you commune with Me in Spirit, there is just Spirit, for that is what I am and what you truly are, and all perceptions that might be compared with your earthly senses of sight and feelings, or even sound, are not totally true. In the strictest sense of the word, the perception of Love and perception of Light are steps to help you enter the courtyard, or the garden, before the palace—before the mansion where the Father dwells. The unending Love, and the brilliant and blinding Light, beckon to you from afar, and you follow them. The Light you follow is as a star leading you homeward, and the Love gives you a feeling of security in your insecure world of identification with your body. But as you return back to My Heart, the time will come when you pass **through** the gateway—beyond the Light and the Love—into resting in Spirit, in Holiness, and in My Peace, where you do also experience a Love, but in a different way—a Love in the realm of Spirit, knowing you rest in My Heart, and that your greatest desire is to extend and create even as I do: in wholeness without any desire yourself to be separate or to create that which is separate.*

And so, the term distortion has been used to describe a free will that was the choice of a will separate from the Father, and a perception of a Light and a Love within these domains that could remind you of your own Source, your own Being, and lead you back even beyond those things that seem to be as a veil across My Being, which as you begin your return, is more than your earthbound consciousness could bear. And these veils are a way of beckoning you to come and pass through, and to go beyond.

Know My child: you rest always in My heart, and at any point in your life you may choose to release your fantasies—your horror fantasies—which will later appear to you to simply have been as a movie that was meant to scare you, but if you had kept your anchor in Me, you would have known it had no reality. I hold you ever in My arms; you are My dear child. I have great joy in you, and as I put My arms around you, it will be easier for you to lay your fantasies aside and know yourself resting in Me—and be content and have a peace that nothing else could give you.

How is God involved in the processes and goings-on in the physical world? Does He care about the activities we get ourselves involved in?

I am involved in every part of your life. Even though these fantasies you created are not of Me—are not My creation and in reality do not exist—yet, in the fantasy, in the mad story of fear and violence—and even the story of a limited joy and love—I am there with you; I participate with you; and even your fantasies could not appear to you to exist or have any form if I were not also there. And so, my child, you encounter Me everyday, everywhere you turn—in each person you see, in each plant or tree you behold, in each animal you see scurrying across your pathway, and also in the breeze. I am always there beyond the form; and the events and situations that arise in your life are opportunities brought to you. Sometimes they may startle you, for you may need a rather strong wake-up call, and then again, the situations that come to you may be so gentle, so sweet, as to touch you on the deepest level of your heart because of their beauty.

So, as you go through your life, begin to seek to trust Me and to release your fears of things. No matter what crops up in your life, see it as an opportunity I have come to present to you—an opportunity to make it easier for you to look through the mask of what it may seem, to see Me there, and then to say, "My Blessed Father, I know not what this means. Help me to experience it as an opportunity to look beyond, to see You there, and in all gentleness to embrace my brothers in every form I see—and in so doing to awaken them to the truth of what they are, and to a recognition of the illusory nature of the interpretations the bodily senses have brought to them."

Are there other techniques or methods besides communing and forgiveness that would assist us in healing the sense of having been abandoned by God?

There are numerous techniques that have been used throughout the ages, some of which are extremely demanding upon you and require enormous patience and ability to focus the mind. I would ask you not to judge against these or your brothers who have benefited from these disciplines, these techniques, but do bear in mind that forgiveness that leads to communion is My gift of an easy way for you to awaken from your sleep—the sleep of your soul—and to stir within you memories of what you truly are and what you knew before the veil of this fantasy appeared to have dropped before your eyes—appeared to have concealed the truth that is there beyond every form. For some of the techniques that have been used are much too difficult for many upon the earth, but I have given you a way that is so easy that most of your brothers, with only a little willingness, will be capable of using and benefiting from it.

And so, I would say to you that if you have some joy in, or fascination with, other techniques, then continue with that, but do not lay aside forgiveness and communing. They are the easiest and the quickest way, as well as the most perfect way, of bringing knowledge to you, and also to your brothers—a double blessing that happens simultaneously, or (better said) two sides of one coin that all happen together. It is not possible for only one side to receive a blessing from this technique, even though in time it may appear to you that one side may possibly receive its blessing more quickly (earlier), but this is not really true. For the benefits—the blessings— of joining in spirit are instantaneous and await your willingness and your desire to accept all these gifts that are piled up before the door of your heart—and that of your brothers— waiting for you to simply open the door and have them fall upon you and cause you to laugh and dance with joy—and give thanks for the Father's perfect solution to your idea of, "How would it be to be separate from God?" and the ensuing fantasy that proved to be a nightmare.

Can the process of returning to full knowledge of our identity as a part of God be hastened, or is it necessarily a long process?

The process is instantaneous, but your understanding—your ability to accept it, to grasp it—may appear to you to take some time, for your limited earth consciousness must first accustom itself to these gifts and the process; and the time needed for this to happen—to come about—depends upon your desire and your willingness to become disentangled from your dream—from your nightmare. And so, do bear in mind that sometimes the worst nightmares are the ones that hasten you along the way, for as you scream in terror at the things you think you behold, then you are much more willing to release your grasp upon this dream of nothingness; whereas, if you are experiencing some soft and gentle aspect of the dream, then you may become slothful, you may tend to doze—to fall asleep and become complacent. Give thanks for all the horrible nightmares that jolt you awake and remind you to ask for something else, for they are your blessing—a blessing from Me.

Behind every hideous image, every terrifying situation, every agonizing illness, I stand there always beckoning to you, asking of you, "Open your eyes and realize where you are, that you truly rest in My arms, and that this awful nightmare is just a horror story." You have nothing to fear, nothing whatsoever. I am your loving Father; you came forth from My Heart; you are a part of Myself; and you are never abandoned. Always remember; just always remember! Speak to Me; talk to Me; ask of Me. Allow yourself to feel that you are in My embrace and have no place to go, no journey to take—for you rest in Me. And as you remain on earth, there is only a purpose of aiding your brothers—not indulging in the dream or a thought of something that cannot be, but remaining in order to help your brothers—to take them by the hand. Allow Me through you to embrace them and comfort them as you bring them back to Me.

How can we help or assist humanity as a whole in this process of remembering our true identity?

Each time you approach one of your brothers in spirit, speaking to him gently of the holiness you behold in his heart, and of your appreciation for him and his allowing Me through him to bless you, you bring the whole of that which had turned away and become fascinated with the story, the fantasy. Each one, being a part of the whole as he is brought back, causes a stronger tug upon the hearts of the others. However, you may also, in your periods of quietness and devotion as you come to Me, open your heart and say, "Blessed Father, I offer my love for all of my brothers, all who feel lost. I may have never seen or heard of them individually, but I offer it on this day, and I ask You to take this love that I offer, that I bring before the altar to You, and give it to them. Give to each one—even those who may not yet be asking for it. Do not allow one single brother to be without some part of my gift." In so doing you also assist the whole in a different way. Also, when you hear of events of terrible wars in other countries, you may just embrace the whole of the inhabitants of those countries. Offer them love and speak to them of the purity within, and know, my child, that in whatever way you do this, every child is blessed in some way.

And as situations arise in your life, you may simply come before Me and say, "Father, speak to me. Give me the ideas. Tell me how I can be your vessel for the maximum benefit of all involved." And I will put the ideas into your mind, which could simply be just to offer love in the moment, but in some cases it could also be to take part in some action (some deed), to go some place, to speak some words, or even to send a donation to someone who is also engaged in assisting your brothers. Be always open to accept whatever I may place before you, the thoughts I may place in your mind. Be open to feeling and knowing My embrace—My arms around you as I take you and lead you into whatever process or situation that may be helpful to the whole of the Sonship—My beloved Child.

Is bringing comfort in simple ways assisting truly or simply reinforcing the sense of identity with the body and the feeling of helplessness?

The extent of the benefit depends upon your intention, and you have been told before: "Set your intention everyday, all through the day, to be an empty vessel and to allow Me through you to bless your brothers." So, if you have set your intention, and you look upon the purity within the hearts of your brothers, then you will know, as I prompt you as to what to do. But remember: each kind and loving deed has much greater effect if it is preceded by an acknowledgment of purity—of holiness—in the hearts of your brothers, and if it falls on the heels of such, it has the effect of awakening your brothers on a deeper level to turn within and recognize the gift you have placed on the altar of their hearts. If you fail to offer this forgiveness, this experience of communing, this acknowledgment and appreciation of the beauty of Myself in your brother's heart, then it is possible that your kind and loving deed may be perceived as an act of pity, rather than an act of love, which would then be perceived as your acknowledging and believing that your brothers are in a state of need, of imbalance and imperfection; and therefore, you would be supporting their illusions.

So, always come first to Me and allow Me to inspire you as to those loving deeds on the earthly level—those kind words, the assistance you might give, and the smile—and then know that these gifts come forth from the real gift, the deeper gift, the initial gift; and therefore, they add unto it and make it easier for your brothers—for they are then receiving gifts on different levels, some of which they may be aware of, and some of which they are not. In this way your brothers are assisted in the best possible way, for you are acknowledging their whole being—including the body with which they are temporarily identifying themselves. And they become aware of and accept your recognition of that purity within them—and that they come forth from the Father's Heart and are ever undefiled.

As our stay on earth extends and the body begins to decline, is there a purpose in lingering? If not, is there a way to release ourselves into Spirit gently without the usual infirmity and suffering?

Rest in Me. Always desire and ask to be helped to be aware, all through the day, that you rest in Me, and ask the Father that you may be always kept pure—an empty vessel through which blessings may be given to your brothers. And each time you have served as a vessel, come back to the Father and say, "Is there another one whom you could bless through me? I offer myself, and I ask you to take care of the vessel so that it may always be capable—that it may have the strength and have the means to sustain it—and that it may be Your vessel of Love and Joy—the vessel through which my brothers come to a state of awakening." Then trust, my child, that the body—the earthly body, which at this point is your vehicle (your temporary, limited identity)—and all its needs will be taken care of. And as you desire to be of such assistance, to be a vessel, then trust that the aging process of the body will not hinder you in doing that which I would have you do. And when the time has come to lay this body aside, give thanks for it, and there will be no reason that you might linger in a state in which you can no longer be a vessel, for those who do linger in this state are still so identified with the body that they are not ready to release it.

Trust, trust Me totally! Give no thought to the body's needs or its processes, except minimal attention such as is needed on the earth level, and trust Me to take care of all the rest. If you have fear of the body, declining energies, or illnesses, then you have lost the vision, you have allowed your gaze to wander in another direction—you have identified, not with Me, but with that which is transitory—and then you will have fear. But as you recognize that your gaze has wandered, you need only turn back towards the Light, and know yourself springing into My Heart and being fully aware of that oneness—knowing that you belong there—and all fears subside, for there is truly nothing to fear.

How can we overcome the feeling of lack?

The feeling of lack is the result of identification with your body on earth—and identification with the feeling of being separate from God. When you rest in Me, and you know My Love enveloping you—when you know that you are not apart from Me—there is no feeling of lack, for there is nothing that you could possibly need. Then as you go forth into the world and there appear to be certain needs for things you might wish to do or for taking care of the body, you need only ask Me. Ask Me to provide that which is appropriate, and if there is something you might prefer, then say, "Father, if it is Your Will, arrange this, but if it is not in the highest good of myself and my brothers, then take this wish or desire of mine and convert it into a desire for that which is true and holy, and that which would benefit me and my brothers in the best way possible.

Is there a closing message from Jesus?

I walk with you everyday and have great joy in you—and also great joy in your recognition and acknowledgment of My Presence. I also have great joy in your desire to be the Father's empty vessel and go forth, even as I did, speaking on various levels to your brothers of their true identity, of the beauty which they are—speaking to them of this, brushing aside any clouds or veils that may appear before that true identity, and not accepting that image they may be projecting to you (never accepting that they are inadequate, in need, or lacking in some way—lacking wholeness or completeness). Look with great fervor and love upon the purity in their hearts! Focus upon it! Then you will only barely hear what they say and only barely see, as if it were a light image, that which is projected towards you. You will embrace them and speak to them of your love, and in so doing, you lift them from the depths of that pit of murky darkness in which they may perceive themselves as dwelling. You lift them away from that, for in parting the veil—removing the clouds of darkness and allowing that brilliant holiness that glows there to inspire you, to lift you up—you also are lifting them with you and causing them to lessen their grip on these illusions—and to release their fear, or even their self-loathing and disdain.

As you speak to them and they recognize the purity of your message, they will know that you speak of truth—deep within they will know. And the time will come when even their earthly consciousness will recognize that which you speak—and that with which you envelop them—and they will know that they have received a blessing from the Father. So, go forth, My brother—My brother in whom I have great joy—knowing that I am always there with you wherever you are. And speak to Me. Speak to Me of the joy you have in recognizing your brothers, and also speak to Me of what you may perceive as certain things that may be needed. Then release them quickly to Me and know that I and the Father are one, and We arrange all things. Go forth always knowing My arms are around you, and even thinking that you hear My footsteps—listening so that you may hear them—beside you, for you may hear them along with your own and know that you are never alone.

COMMUNING WITH A BROTHER

COMMUNING WITH A BROTHER

It was brought to my attention that a teenage boy (we'll call him "Andrew") had succumbed to peer pressure and allowed himself to participate in an unkind and illegal act against one of his schoolmates. I desired to commune with him and offer myself as the Father's vessel for all that might be appropriate and needed at that time. I approached him in spirit and asked the Father to inspire me as to what to say and do.

The Vessel speaks:

My blessed, holy brother, I come to you in great joy. I come to you to tell you of the beauty that I behold in your heart, and to tell you of my gratitude that you allow me to look upon this. I come to remind you that you come forth from the Heart of God as a pure and blessed child—a child of holiness—

come into the world with a great mission—a mission that begins with your own recognition of that which is within your heart. I come to remind you of your mission to awaken your brothers—to participate in the process in this great time of harvest (to assist and be sure that not one single soul who calls out will fail to have a response). I come to remind you that across the heart of each one there may be a veil—there may appear to be the form of the body, or even the personality—but the veil is very thin. I come to remind you that the Father has given you a gift, and it is in your hands. Reach forth to the heart of each brother, and you will be allowed to lift that veil gently and slowly—not to frighten him, but to allow him a glimpse of that light within you. You have come forth to assist.

Consider that all the experiences in your life come about as a way of preparing you to understand and recognize your purpose and your role in being here. Even now in this moment I would ask you, as you allow me to put my arms around you and to give you my embrace, that you also allow me to take you with me before the Father. We come to Him, and we say, "Oh, Blessed Father, bless us together, two brothers who come before you and who say, 'We accept in great joy this charge, this assignment; and we ask you to help us to always recognize the opportunities, and help us to always acknowledge your Holiness in each heart.'"

And now, my dear brother, Andrew, let us look upon the heart of this one who appeared to have led you astray, the one who instigated this incident that has brought some concern. Look upon his heart with me and know that there within is a Joy; there is a Light; there is a Love—there is the Father who can be discovered by us. Let us look upon this together and say, "Blessed brother, we come to you. We bring you an embrace from the Father. We know that all these things you have done were incidents of calling out for a Love that you miss, that you need—a Love you feel you do not have—and you were just not aware of the appropriate way to call for It. We accept your method; we recognize it, and we offer appreciation for the beauty within you. And now Andrew and I come to you, one on each side; we spread out our arms; and we envelop you into our hearts." And now we offer a prayer: "Blessed Father, we thank you for this one. We thank you for his call of love. We thank you that you have brought him to us, and us to him. We thank you that he allows us to embrace him and to be a part of his awakening. And now we lift him up into Your arms and say, 'Prepare for him each day gently that which will bring him further in his own recognition of his pathway and his assignment on earth. And should at any moment he forget and have a need for love, for an embrace and acknowledgment of his true identity, tap us on the heart, Andrew and myself, tap us on the heart; remind us that this one is calling out in this moment; and say to us, "Come again. Put your arms around him and know that in embracing him, you have opened yourselves wholly to Me and My embrace, for you receive Me and My embrace by embracing your brother."' And now we lift him into Your arms and ask Your richest blessings upon him." And bless us now, Andrew and myself, two brothers who would go back into the world and say, "Help us, Father, each day to recognize every opportunity. Help us not to forget. Take away all fear that might have been in our hearts of what our other brothers might say or think. Help us to remember this embrace we have had and know that it is much more important than any thoughts our brothers might have or express. Help us each day—in the morning as we begin the day, in the evening as the day comes to a close—to remember to come to You and say, 'Thank you, Blessed Father, for this day and for the opportunities our brothers have.' And so, we ask You to keep us empty, keep us clean—pure and empty vessels so that we may always be ready for the next brother who comes along." And now, in departing I give you my embrace, dear brother, Andrew, and I say, "Come to me—come to me in spirit. Walk with me as I take my walks. Come to me and talk to me—when you have a need to speak to a friend, speak to me. It is with great joy that I await your call. I thank you that you have allowed me to enter into your heart and embrace the Father there. And I ask the Blessed Jesus to always walk beside you, to talk to you, to lead you wherever you need to go, to protect you from those things that might cause you to stumble (to lift you up above them), and to help you to bless those around you—be the vessel through which every single student in your school is blessed so that they may also know they walk in Love and Light—in Holiness—and are here for the purpose of extending this, and of recognizing it and appreciating it in others. I bless you, my dear brother, and I thank you for accepting my love and giving me your own."

MESSAGE FOR A FRIEND

MESSAGE FOR A FRIEND

What is the soul blueprint of _____?

This son was created out of My Heart with an intense capability of extending love and dancing in the Light of the Spirit. This one also has the capability of being of assistance to other brothers, and in order to do so it is necessary that he experience some of the things that other brothers are having to endure, so that he may better identify with, understand, and have a greater patience with them. He has come into the earth at this time so that he may participate in the time of harvest and be of assistance to those who may just simply need a gentle nudging—just a little assistance—a touching of the spirit in order to awaken in them the knowledge that there is a possibility to request to be a part of this time of harvest. He is preparing himself by experiencing these things, as well as also being confronted with the ego, which is associated with the earth plane, so that he may then go beyond any personal desires and also release unto the Father any fear he might have of suffering—or death itself—knowing that he rests in the Father's arms, that all is well, and that each experience that comes to him is a part of the process of his own unfolding, and in preparation for making him an empty vessel through which the Father can express upon the earth. Therefore, it is fitting that he should, as he approaches the Father and the Master, Jesus, give thanks that all is well, all is under control, and that he will be given the experiences that will help him to better serve.

_____ is encouraged to have faith and to know—to accept—that the Master does walk beside him and has great love for him. Actually, as the Master walks beside him, He has his arms around the shoulders of _____. And in believing that the Master is there, then he is opening the door to experiencing it; and the experience will come—the knowledge of the Presence of the Master will come. But also he needs to understand that in the process here upon earth it is important that our endurance be tested, that he must show he really desires to have these spiritual experiences and to have the knowledge of the Father and of the Master, and that he is *willing to endure and continue to believe, in spite of what might appear at the present to be a lacking in those experiences—what might be compared to dwelling in a desert land. But as time goes on he will come to see, experience, and know the fullness of the Spirit. And that beautiful Light that is in his heart will shine forth as he allows the door to his heart to remain open and bless those around him.*

*_____ is asked to consider and accept that those he comes into contact with—those in his workplace—are also sent to him, even now at this point, as brothers whom he can serve; and that he should, in spite of how they may appear to him and what their attitudes may seem to be, always remember to look beyond the mask of the personality for that Light. For truly as he comes to believe that the Father is come to him as each of these persons, seemingly wearing a mask—yet the Father **is** there, and as he concentrates upon the Presence of the Father, the Spirit of the Father in each one—his heart will then open, and he will experience that Presence. And he will bless those, even though they may be making his life difficult in some ways. As time goes on they will themselves, on some level deep within, recognize that he is allowing the Father to* *bless them through him, and their attitude about him will change. So, what is the blueprint of the soul? The blueprint is to allow this beautiful and lively, energetic Light in his heart to shine forth—not to close down the doors of the heart or the mind, but to open them—to fling them open—so that the Light within him, which is so beautiful, may shine forth and embrace all those around him. For truly he is himself a part of anchoring the Light of the Father in the earth, and he is serving a role as being part of the salvation of his brothers.* [Speaking now directly to the soul] *And so, my gentle brother, know that Love and Light are your birthright—they are already within you. The only thing that is lacking is opening those doors as wide as possible, so that the Light flows through you, and you are yourself a vessel, which is blessed by the flowing of the Light as it goes through you and blesses those around you. You have a calling to a holy task, and you are encouraged to accept this calling without reservation—without having any personal goals or aspirations that would be between you and the Father's mission for you.*

_____ has asked Jerry to pray for him and has been reading Jerry's writings; however, he has a problem following the principles and putting them into practice. Can any help be given?

*The problem of not experiencing the Presence of the Father in those whom he would visualize in front of him lies in remembrances of past experiences—in allowing those remembrances to be so strong as to engender some fear and cause his heart, in a gesture of protection, to close down. He is encouraged to believe that it **is** the Father's Spirit there, and that, certainly in a time of meditation when he is not in the physical presence of these other brothers or sisters, there is nothing to fear—that what he is remembering, and which causes some fear, is something of the past, which is no longer—it exists no longer. It is a remembrance and should be released, for even these remembrances are interpretations, and simply perceptions. If he will truly try to believe that the person he is visualizing is the Father or our Master, Jesus, come to him simply wearing a mask, and that the mask can be gently drawn away as if opening a veil, then he can truly gaze upon Holiness and Pure Light, and he can know an unconditional Love that can only be from the Father, flowing forth, for that mask will become so invisible that he forgets about its* *being there. And truly, once this is experienced, he will look upon those whom he visualizes in his prayer, meditation, and devotional period as opportunities, and he will rejoice in the fact that he can go to them again to seek his blessings in their hearts, as well as allow the blessings of the Father to flow through him to them. He is encouraged to continue, to persevere in doing this, and not to be discouraged by what would be thought of as a failure, for truly, the key is already in the door and has been turned. He is now on the threshold, and the opportunity is there to simply push against the door so that it opens and these experiences flow forth upon him as a waterfall of Light and blessings—and he may laugh and rejoice, and give thanks that he is here upon the earth at this time and can participate in this time of harvest.*

How can he be helped in dealing with past experiences with the mother?

There are several ways, and in the beginning it might be helpful simply to think about the mother and realize that there was also a veil across her consciousness—she was experiencing some problems of her own and cannot be held totally *accountable for some of her deeds and her reactions. And then as he allows his thoughts to go in this direction, he can feel a compassion for the mother welling up from within the heart and an ability to understand that she perhaps did the very best she could at the time, considering the level of her realizations and the problems she was facing in her life. As compassion comes upon him, then truly he can extend his arm in love and touch his mother in spirit, and say, "I'm sorry. I didn't understand, but now I do, and truly I forgive you. I ask you to forgive my earlier inabilities to understand. Now accept that I extend my love to you, and I also desire **your** embrace."*

How can _____ be helped with physical problems? Does he need certain therapies?

While dwelling upon earth it is certainly appropriate to take advantage of different therapies that may be offered, for the physical body is very dense, and weaknesses—even condensations of crystals or knotting up of the muscles—do require at times help on the physical level. Bear in mind that this is not the only assistance he should be given. It should be done in conjunction with seeking to release the fears—fears that have come from the past, and fears and anxieties of the present—for truly the body does express the consciousness on the earth level. As these fears are released and Light and Love are allowed to flow, then the body is less likely to become tense and to cause pain. As the other therapies are used to release those tensions that are the result of past anxieties and fear, then a feeling of well-being can come—and will come—upon even the personality and the physical vehicle at this time.

How can he come to know the Presence of Jesus?

As he reads scriptures from the Bible, he should visualize that he was there in the various scenes in which the Master took part, and that he also had the opportunity to address the Master, to speak to Him—to ask questions and to receive guidance. And in doing so, he can, as he is imagining these scenes, just simply go ahead and ask his own questions, believing that he truly is in the Presence of the Master and accepting that the Master will give answers—not always in that moment, but He will give us answers when the time is appropriate. And as _____ reads these stories and imagines the Presence of the Master, surely he will begin to feel the Presence of Him in that scene. And as this comes about he will then realize that he can feel the Master and His Presence as he goes about his duties on earth. It requires a certain amount of imagination and accepting the promises of the Master, for He has truly told us that He is in our hearts and He is always with us—even unto the end. We should not doubt these promises, but accept them as true—even today in this time.

What can be given to assist _____'s spiritual development?

As doubts and fears come upon him, he should pause, when the opportunity presents itself, and accept that he exists because the Father is within him; that truly the Father, who created him, is a Father of Love; and that by imagining this, he comes before the Presence of the Father (or that when he is out walking, the Master walks beside him)—that this truly does take place, and as he accepts to believe it, the experience of that Presence will be known. But it takes a conscious and deliberate act of his own consciousness—a discipline within him—to do this, and it would certainly be helpful to assign a certain time every day to do this without fail, and not simply imagine that one can just read spiritual books and have it happen on its own. One must put forth a certain effort—one must attempt to accept and to believe, and one must also make a point of setting aside some time to do this.

What conditions in his life can be changed and what is required of him?

It is required of him to participate in the mundane life on earth. What can be changed is his perception of the conditions of his life. Rather than dwelling upon the experience of stress brought about by demands placed upon him by the job, dwelling upon the way some individuals may treat him, or the lack of recognition for his attempts to always do an excellent job—by allowing himself to release these things rather than dwelling upon them—he should dwell upon thoughts of his mission to extend love, and remind himself from day to day that the job itself, and relationships, are opportunities the Father has placed before him—opportunities to allow the Father through him to bless those around him. And truly the

Father will bring to him those who are in need of a blessing—those who are in need of an experience of being accepted without reservation, and who are in need of a love that has no personal gain as its purpose—and as he does this, then the perception of the job will change, and he will see that the Father has placed him where he is because there are those around him who can be blessed. This is and should be his goal. He should accept this as his higher purpose, and realize that when some mundane gift might pass him by, it is not that he is being slighted, but in some cases those worldly gifts might have been a distraction—might have delayed him in his own process on his path, and also might have caused him to neglect to extend a blessing to someone else. For these mundane gifts of life can be a distraction, allowing one, or causing one, to neglect his true mission on earth.

Is there a closing message for _____?

Walk forth in the Light into the world, allowing It to beam forth from you—allowing your brothers to see in expressions on your face, in your countenance, and in the tone of your voice, that you are anchored in the Love and Light of the

*Father (that you are truly here to bless, and that your brothers and sisters have nothing to fear), so that they would give thanks that they may come to you and receive blessings, and may not feel that they walk in a desert land and must fight for those things that are needed for life itself. For truly they can receive blessings, just as two thousand years ago those who knew Jesus, our Master, received blessings from Him. Walk in that pathway. Ask Him to be in you—to be you walking the earth. And it **can** happen—it **will** happen—and you will recognize that this is your salvation—this is your happiness—and that you can feel at home under any circumstances in which the Father should place you.*

MESSAGE FOR THE VESSEL

MESSAGE FOR THE VESSEL

How is spiritual knowledge made use of within a mundane life?

Life on earth requires that you look to the Father moment by moment, that you learn to accept that you of yourself really know nothing, for you do not know how to interpret or understand the circumstances, the events, of the life around you. This is a learning process that may take some time, but one must learn to always turn to the Father and say, "Show me Your Will in this moment so that I not go astray or make a detour," as well as (and it is equally important), "so that my brothers not be harmed or hindered, but rather be helped and assisted," and therefore, be looking for a deeper understanding of life and looking for guidance. One must understand that gain in the mundane sense of the word is to be released, and understand that extending Love is the highest ideal—and should also be the purpose that is chosen in each moment. It is important to keep in mind that the personality in its ignorance very often makes mistakes and will then later see that its choices were not wise; and then as this realization comes upon the person, upon that soul, that he or she not get lost in guilt, but rather say simply, "I have made a false choice. I choose again in this moment, and I release the other choice. I ask the Father's richest blessings upon those whom I may have neglected, or even have offended. I desire to recognize the Spirit of the Father within each one of those. I desire to stretch forth my arms and embrace them, knowing that it is the Spirit of the Father I am embracing. And I now consider the mistaken choice as simply bringing my attention to an opportunity of communing with the Father and His children that I might otherwise have missed, had I not made the blunder and then for just a slight second, or even a moment, felt guilty. **This** *was the impetus that opened the door to a miracle of an embrace of Holiness that transported me beyond all perceptions of any sort of lack or imperfection, or being victimized, and, therefore, there was Holiness in that moment because of the outcome!"*

Always bear in mind that you should set your purpose each day, all through the day, when you have a moment to reflect—set your purpose to recognize your Father, His Spirit, in each one; and to be a vessel, an empty and pure vessel, through which blessings from the Father can flow to your brothers around you. And then never allow yourself to be depressed should you in some moment forget this, but simply say again to the Father, "Always remind me. I would not that my brothers and sisters be harmed in any way or feel slighted. Even though perhaps my personality may reach the end of its patience and express itself impatiently, may it simply be in that moment what my brothers and sisters may need themselves, but may it not bring harm to them. And as I recognize the situation, may I offer to them an embrace of Love that will bring an even greater blessing than any they might otherwise have received."

Is there anything more to be added on how one stays anchored in Spirit and functions in the outer world?

As time goes on and you accept your mission on earth, it is good, and it is appropriate, that you will gradually reach a point where you will more and more often think of the Father and His Love, and you will try not to get so caught up in the things of earth that have no deeper meaning—so that you will then remember more and more often to just simply whisper to the Father, or to your Blessed Brother, Friend, and Master, Jesus, "I love You. I adore You. Be in me. Express through me." And as you do this more and more often, Light becomes anchored upon earth through you, and you truly become the Father's vessel. But certainly as you first begin to be interested in things of a higher spiritual nature, you must discipline yourself by setting certain times during the day (and not letting anything else come in between or interfere) in which you take a few moments to quietly look to the Father and embrace your brothers. This is the beginning. Then it becomes a habit. And then it becomes your life.

What are some exercises to use in order to learn to apply spiritual knowledge in mundane life?

Should any of your brothers and sisters come to you—even though not intentionally coming to you for that purpose (just simply speaking to you, confiding in you)—even then there is an implied request for help. Then ask the Father and your Blessed Master to show you, to put into your mind the thoughts, to put upon your lips the words, of things that would be helpful to them. These things can range from simply suggesting to someone who is a bit frustrated to take a deep breath and just smile (just for the sake of experiencing that opening of the heart when one smiles), and then putting into their minds the thoughts that the one, or ones, who have offended them were perhaps somewhat deluded, were not seeing clearly, and that they should be excused (reminding them that sometimes they may have done the same thing); to simply speaking to another person and expressing appreciation for some of that person's most heartfelt and light-filled thoughts and expressions, or for their talents—to compliment them. This is a step in the direction towards communing with the Father in your brothers and sisters—to simply begin by looking for something positive, and then to strive to bring out the positive, rather than bring out the worst, in them.

But always look to the Father and ask Him. He will place those thoughts into your mind and will direct your mind away from thoughts that you on a personality level might have thought were best. For there may be times when you feel there is a situation where, unless the perfect thought, the perfect words, are expressed, you will have the opposite effect. And sometimes the exercise for you may simply be to smile and place your hand upon the shoulder of another person, or to sit down in quiet and extend Love—and ask the Father to bless you with His Love coming forth from their hearts. For as you do that you are encouraging them to open their hearts, and sometimes this is even done better without speaking words, or giving ideas and teachings that could bring about arguments. This way you allow the Father to present to them in a way that is perfect for them, and, therefore, to open a door that would have remained bolted if you had not asked the Father for the perfect way by simply saying, "I really desire that my brother or sister be blessed in some way this day, even through me, even if I may not be aware of it." The important thing is the blessing: touching the heart, awakening it to a joy that it has forgotten—and yet a joy that would certainly attract its attention. And then, you may be surprised—some brother may come to you and say, "You know, an hour ago I was really frustrated; I was so filled with anger; and suddenly, I can't explain it, there was a cooling off. And now

I feel a peace in my heart. I wonder what happened." So can you be the Father's vessel, and so can you perfectly express your function on earth.

Is there more that can be given as to what might be the spiritual function on the job and how to better do the job so that others are blessed in the best and most complete way?

Each day should be begun with a prayer. Each day should be dedicated to blessing your brothers—allowing the Father through you to bless them and not requesting or requiring that you always know about this, for this could in some way inflate the ego. Simply begin the day with this prayer, and then when you reach a point in your work where a decision has to be made, rather than trying to weigh it in the scales of rational and analytical process, simply say, "Father, show me. Show me which way the scales fall for the ultimate and best good of my brother." And realize that there are times when showering mundane gifts on your brothers could deprive them of lessons they also need to learn, because there are times when the idle mind gets the soul in trouble. And yet, always desire relief for your brothers. Just allow the Father to show you the way, and be not dismayed when the process takes more time than you think you have available for that particular process, that particular person.

Accept that the Father will certainly provide for His vessel, and when there are requirements upon you, you may spend a whole day working to help one person, and then the next day have three very easy assignments that are the Father's pouring forth His blessings upon you in order to enable you to remain in your position and help those who are extremely needy—and who also may require a bit of time. Bear in mind that your Blessed Brother and Master has devoted much time to you—time on earth, and also time in other realms (although it is a different kind of time, it is a process)—and he has extended much Love to you and helped you; therefore, is it not your privilege, as well as duty, to go forth desiring to be like unto Him and to extend a hand to help those who are not yet able to do all that is needed for themselves? For truly you cannot bask in the Father's Light and Love knowing there are those who are crying out, and all you have to do is go forth and extend your arms to them saying, "Father, bless through me." Remember this everyday, all through the day. Extend blessing to those who work around you, for there are those who also need a touch of Love and an experience of Light. You can also touch their souls and bring joy to them in the process of taking care of the requirements of your job. Do not look upon the job as a chore, but an opportunity, a **blessing**—*a blessing in the form of opportunity to accomplish your mission and not risk coming to the end of the earth life and saying, "My God! How I have wasted the time on earth. Look at all those who were extending their arms to me, and I passed by and said, 'May God help you,' and then left them in dire straits."*

Is there something more the vessel needs to do to make attunement for these messages better?

You have chosen well! You have chosen to come before My Presence, and you have chosen to ask for the assistance of your Holy Brother, known to you as Jesus. This is a holy and perfect process, and it (as you so well know) has served very well. It serves you and your brothers, for you know that in coming in this way (and also with the assistance of this beautiful and gentle sister of yours), you come into My Presence—

you come to know that you rest in My Presence—and you know this Holy Light That is yourself (That is within you) and this Love—you experience and know this as you come in this way. Your part, your role, in assisting your brothers (and as being a companion with your Holy Brother, Jesus), and the part of your dear sister, is very much appreciated by Myself and by My Son, Jesus—your Holy Companion. We delight in your coming before Us and asking (over and over again) for more and more to help your brothers. All is well. You have chosen well. And so has your assistant (your companion in this process) chosen well, and My Hand rests upon her in all that she does in assisting others. Know this, beautiful child, We are always with you.

A question was asked about what the vessel might do after retirement.

There will be more and more opportunities to commune with your brothers on different levels (some face to face in using words), and you will accept to be the Father's vessel through which all sorts of blessings come to your brothers—words of wisdom, a Love flowing forth, an experience of the Light and

Holiness of the Father flowing through you. And as your brothers come to you, you will recognize that there are those who first of all need to hear you say, "I understand because I have also had a similar experience." And when they say to you, "I have not acted in a good and proper way," then you can also remember that there were times when you yourself did not, and you can say, "But that doesn't matter. That was in the past. Let me tell you: I always put that behind me and allow it to only be a reminder to me to always look to the Father, and a reminder that I can only live now in this moment and look forth into the future—and allow the past to be stepping stones, not stumbling blocks." And when they understand that you yourself have felt their agonies, their anxieties, and you have known their pain, then they will trust you, and they will listen further as you suggest to them that which the Father puts into your mind, which is held for them already in store—ways to turn their lives in a different direction (to a life expressing Light and extending Love).

And then you will rejoice that you yourself went through those things—went through those experiences that at times brought you agony, brought you depression, made you want to leave the earth—because this prepared you to be the Father's vessel whom He could send out into the byways of earth to those who would not need or understand teachings, preaching, or precepts, but who simply first need an embrace. For you now know that everyone on the earth needs something at sometime; that what is the greatest need in the moment is what the Father will present to you; and that it is important for you to realize that you take care of that which is given in the moment, and not try to jump into things that are perhaps best kept for a later date.

A question was asked as to what could be done to help an incapacitated person.

Acknowledge the great love that she extends to you each day. Reach forth and touch her, embrace her. Not only tell her that you love her, but also tell her how happy you are to have her in your life. In your quiet moments speak to her soul, express your appreciation for the opportunity of participating in this life with her, and ask that you be given the strength to carry on, and the means to provide. Ask the Father to help you to make each day as easy as possible and as filled with joy as possible for her, and also, when her time comes to be graduated from earth into higher realms, that you be helped to extend Love to her and provide everything possible to make that process as easy, as effortless, as filled with joy, as possible, so that she may never know a moment of feeling in need or feeling alone, and may rush into the arms of those awaiting her, gently leaving the body with no sense of pain or regret. Ask always that the Father's Will be done and that you be helped to never neglect in providing all blessings that can be helpful to her.

A question was asked about changes that would come for her in the near future, and what could be done to help her when changes occur?

It is important to realize that when a soul comes to earth, there are certain events and patterns it has accepted that are in accordance with the Father's Will (and that also may not be changed), but you should always ask the Father to help you to be there and be available, and to do your part in bringing forth any harmonious change—any change that would bring life and joy, and change that would bring an opportunity for her to laugh, which she does so well, and to extend her hands to touch and caress. And bear in mind that when you ask for this, you could very well be having effect upon the changes that come upon her. Do not ask to always know in advance, but ask that you be helped to be willing to accept what comes; that when you allow the love to flow through you, there will be nothing lacking; and that only that which is required for a higher purpose will come about. Now rest in the assurance of this, and that the time will come—a time of change for you and a time of change for her. Look upon this as the Father's blessing. Be not filled with sorrow when her departure comes, but give thanks for all the experiences you have had with her; and know that whenever you ask the Father each day, He will provide the way for that which is best, and then you will be able to accept whatever may come.

Is there a closing message for the vessel?

Be assured, the provisions for the journey have already been placed there for you. You need have no fear of lack, and no fear of there being any failure to do what the Father has placed before you, so long as it is your desire to do so. Trust totally and accept every blessing that is offered, no matter how it may come wrapped—how it may appear—for even those situations that would seem to interfere and interrupt what might have already been planned are holy occurrences, and are the Father's way of leading you to a direction where Love can be extended and hope can be brought into the soul of another who has fear and sees no light, no opportunities, no doors that may be opened. You have only one function and mission on earth, and that is to be the Father's empty vessel, and when you desire that within your heart, He takes responsibility for everything, and you may walk forth into the world bringing Light and Love, and allowing it to flow through and bless all those around you. There is no other fulfillment, no other goal—no other reason to be here—and all changes the Father may bring about are truly His Will and His way of blessing you and your brothers, so rejoice each day, be grateful for the opportunities, and strive always not to neglect one single brother or sister.

Go forth in the Light, consciously choosing the Light and knowing not only that you are blessed, but also being aware of the great responsibility that comes with the knowledge and experience of the Father that has been bestowed upon you. It was your choice to come, and it was your choice to serve. You have been blessed, and so, go forth, giving thanks each day for what presents itself, and also knowing deep within your heart that when you set your purpose and you ask of the Father, there are no mishaps—that what comes into your experience is for a purpose. It may at first seem to your personality to be an annoyance, to bring about delay and frustration, but then, if you listen quietly within, you will realize: it is just the Father directing your footsteps and showing you which direction to take at the fork in the road, and also the Father come upon earth as you (because you allow it) to gather unto Himself those who are wandering, and lost, and confused—those who call out for help and those who do not know to consciously call out, but who express themselves in ways that you should interpret as a call for help.

Go forth in the knowledge of the great responsibility you have, and also giving thanks that you have the opportunity to be one of those who is blessed with a mission on earth, and desiring that your experience on earth might extend in time as long as the Father has any use for your vesselship in this earth life—never asking, "Father, take me unto Yourself," but always asking, "Father, is there another experience, is there another soul You can touch? Take me to him or her. Bring them to me, and help me that I always welcome them in gentleness and in Love—that I allow You bless them, and ask that the blessing leave an indelible imprint upon their souls: that it be a blessing that attracts them to the Light." Know, my dear child, that you are ever cared for. You need have no fear. You need simply do what is put in front of you and take those ideas given to you, for sometimes those ideas may be a means of opening a door. Open the door and place no requirements upon that door. Ask not that the Father explain to you. Ask not, require not, that you see the results. Just ask in simplicity and humility that your brothers be blessed, and know that by doing so you have made the highest choice you could possibly make on earth. Now go forth in blessings of Light and Love, and always know, I am in your heart and guide you every step of the way, for I dwell in you as you allow it—and then I am on earth expressing through an empty vessel who allows Me to be recognized by those who are ready to recognize Me, so that they may rejoice in Me and choose to also assist in accepting a mission of helping other brothers.

ANOTHER BOOK BY THE AUTHOR

DWELL IN LOVE I
Messages for those of the heart

Jerry K. Paul

Jerry Paul asked God and Jesus for messages for those of the heart in order to inspire and instruct them as to the best way to commune with Divine Presence and discover that Presence in others. The first chapter consists of 211 daily, inspirational messages for use as devotional material. The remainder of the book consists of longer messages in answer to questions asked about healing, service, suffering, forgiveness, sacrifice, praying, how to care for the sick, the current world situation, etc. The main theme of the book is becoming an empty vessel through which God can extend unconditional love.

ANOTHER BOOK BY THE AUTHOR

DWELL IN LOVE II
The Journey of Return

Jerry K. Paul

In *Dwell in Love II: The Journey of Return,* Jerry Paul tells of some of the experiences he has had in prayer and the results of praying for people by communing with the Spirit of God in them. He gives the steps of the way of praying that has worked so well for him. There are also messages on suffering, vicarious suffering, and the spiritual vibrations of about fifty crystals and stones. He shares his remembrance of a reluctance to come to earth and how a talk with Jesus changed his mind.

ORDER FORM

Please print

Name: _____

Address: _____

City: _____ State/Province: _____

Country: _____ Postal Code: _____

Telephone: (_____) _____

Please send me _____ copies of *Dwell in Love I* @ $15.95* per copy.

Please send me _____ copies of *Dwell in Love II* @ $15.95* per copy.

Please send me _____ copies of Dwell in Love III @ $15.95*per copy.

*Add $3.50 for shipping, $1.00 for each additional copy. Alabama residents add 64 cents for state sales tax, those residing in Montgomery County add an additional 40 cents for county sales tax, and those in the city of Montgomery an additional 56 cents for city tax.

Total Amount Enclosed:

$_____(including shipping)

Please make check or money order to:

Isaiah Publications
P.O. Box 31
Pine Level, AL 36065, USA
www.dwellinlove.com